# Heart of the Shepherd
## Character and Life of the Priest

Hegumen Abraam Sleman

*Heart of the Shepherd: Character and Life of the Priest*

© January 2026, Hegumen Abraam Sleman

frsleman@CopticChurch.net

All rights reserved. No part of this publication may be reproduced, stored in a retrieval system, or transmitted in any form or by any means: electronic, mechanical, photocopying, recording, or otherwise, without the prior written permission of the publisher, except in the case of brief quotations embodied in critical articles and reviews.

Updated Second Edition Published: January 2026

ISBN: 978-1-971426-06-8

Unless otherwise mentioned, Scripture quotations are taken from New King James Version®. Copyright © 1982 by Thomas Nelson. Used by permission. All rights reserved.

# Table of Contents

**PREFACE** .................................................................... 5

**CHAPTER 1** ................................................................. 8
    THE SACRED CALL TO PRIESTHOOD ................................................. 8

**CHAPTER 2** ............................................................... 16
    THE PRIEST: A LIVING REFLECTION OF CHRIST ................................. 16

**CHAPTER 3** ............................................................... 20
    PRAYER IN THE PRIEST'S LIFE .................................................. 20

**CHAPTER 4** ............................................................... 27
    THE PRIEST'S CALL TO HOLINESS ................................................ 27

**CHAPTER 5** ............................................................... 34
    THE PRIEST AS A SPIRITUAL FATHER ............................................ 34

**CHAPTER 6** ............................................................... 41
    THE PRIEST'S PASTORAL MINISTRY .............................................. 41

**CHAPTER 7** ............................................................... 49
    TEACHING, PREACHING, AND EVANGELIZING ...................................... 49

**CHAPTER 8** ............................................................... 56
    THE PRIEST AS A MINISTER OF RECONCILIATION ................................ 56

**CHAPTER 9** ............................................................... 64
    THE PRIEST'S LITURGICAL LIFE ................................................. 64

**CHAPTER 10** ............................................................. 71
    THE PRIEST AS THE CELEBRANT OF THE EUCHARIST .............................. 71

**CHAPTER 11** ............................................................. 78
    THE PRIEST AND THE CHURCH: UNITY, AUTHORITY, AND SERVICE ............. 78

**CHAPTER 12** ............................................................. 85
    THE PRIEST'S ROLE IN HIS FAMILY ............................................. 85

**CHAPTER 13** ............................................................. 91

    Spiritual Warfare and Overcoming Trials ................................ 91

**CHAPTER 14.................................................................... 103**

    Bearing the Cross with Christ .............................................. 103

**CHAPTER 15.................................................................... 109**

    The Priest's Spiritual Fruitfulness......................................... 109

**BIBLIOGRAPHY ................................................................. 115**

# Preface

Priesthood is a sacred and profound calling, requiring a life of dedication, personal holiness, and self-sacrifice. From the moment of ordination, the priest enters into a unique and transformative relationship with Christ, the Good Shepherd, who laid down His life for His sheep (John 10:11). This book, *Heart of the Shepherd: Character and Life of the Priest*, explores the depth of this calling, grounded in Scripture, the wisdom of the Church Fathers, and the Church's liturgical tradition.

The reflection of God the Father's love is at the center of the priest's ministry. As Christ revealed the Father's love and care in His earthly ministry (John 14:9-10), so too the priest embodies and reflects this love in his ministry. The priest's role is one of spiritual fatherhood, caring for the souls entrusted to him with the same compassion and dedication that Christ demonstrated. Through the sacraments, preaching, and pastoral care, the priest stands as an intercessor, shepherding God's people with fatherly love. His ministry reflects the very nature of God the Father, who, through Christ, calls all people into communion with Him (John 17:21).

St. Paul captured this spiritual fatherhood when he said, "For though you have countless guides in Christ, you do not have many fathers; for I became your father in Christ Jesus through the Gospel" (1 Corinthians 4:15). In the same way, the priest nurtures the faithful, leading them deeper into communion with the Father, reflecting Christ's ministry in the Church, by the power of the Holy Spirit.

Throughout the years, we have witnessed the profound impact of the priesthood on the lives of both priests and their communities. Priests embody the Father's love through their compassion, wisdom, and humility while also facing the immense challenges of spiritual warfare, personal sacrifice, and pastoral care. In all these struggles, they participate in Christ's mission to reveal the love of God the Father to His children (John 17:6). The priest's life is one of ongoing transformation as he seeks to conform more fully to the image of Christ (Romans 8:29), embracing the grace and joy that come from serving the Lord.

When the priest stands at the holy altar, he offers not only the sacrifice of Christ but also his own life as a living sacrifice (Romans 12:1) and a drink offering (2 Timothy 4:6), embodying the fatherly love of God in service to His people. His role as a spiritual father, guiding the faithful in holiness, reflects God's fatherly love as he nurtures, protects, and shepherds the souls entrusted to him (1 Peter 5:2-3).

This book, *Heart of the Shepherd: The Character and the Life of the Priest*, is written as a reflection on the sacred nature of the priesthood, offering insights into the spiritual character, responsibilities, and life of the priest. Each chapter delves into key aspects of the priest's role, starting with his sacred calling and character formation, progressing through the centrality of teaching, preaching, and the Eucharist, and concluding with the legacy a priest leaves in his community. In every aspect of his ministry, the priest reflects God's fatherly love, guiding the faithful with compassion, patience, and wisdom.

The structure of the book emphasizes that the priest is not alone in his mission. He is part of the larger body of Christ, the Church, and his ministry is intimately connected to the Church's mission of salvation. The priest, in communion with the bishop and the entire Church, fosters unity and guides the faithful in truth and holiness, serving as a spiritual father to his community (Ephesians 4:3).

In writing this book, we have drawn from the rich treasures of Scripture, the teachings of the Church Fathers. The examples of holy priests who have influenced us over the years have profoundly shaped our understanding of this sacred ministry. Our goal is to offer priests a deeper appreciation of their calling, grounded in the Church's rich tradition, while providing theological insights and practical guidance for their daily ministry.

As you read this book, we hope the holy Scriptures will inspire you, the wisdom of the Church Fathers, and the beauty of the liturgy, all of which reveal the dignity and responsibility of the priestly ministry. The priest is called to be a living icon of Christ and a reflection of the Father's love, leading the faithful with humility, sacrifice, and tenderness.

We dedicate this book to all the priests who have faithfully answered the call to serve Christ and His Church. Your sacrifices, love, and unwavering dedication to the Gospel are a testament to the living presence of Christ and the Father's love in the world today. May this book be a source of encouragement, inspiration, and renewal as you continue to carry out the mission of the Good Shepherd.

To those reading this book—whether you are a priest, seminarian, or layperson—we invite you to enter into the heart of the priest's calling. Our prayer is that these pages will deepen your appreciation of the sacred role of the priesthood and its profound impact on the Church and the world.

*Hegumen Abraam Sleman*
*frsleman@CopticChurch.net*
*Jersey City, August 5, 2025*

# Chapter 1

## The Sacred Call to Priesthood

The priesthood is not merely a vocation or profession; it is a divine and sacred calling instituted by God and empowered by the Holy Spirit. From the earliest days of the Church, the priesthood has been recognized as a heavenly ministry, not grounded in human decision but in God's eternal will. It is through the priesthood that the Church experiences the living presence of Christ, for priests serve not only as ministers of sacraments but also as intercessors between God and His people.

## The Divine Origin of Priesthood

The sacred office of the priesthood is deeply rooted in the eternal plan of God, not merely a human institution but a divine calling. Throughout Scripture, God Himself is the one who appoints and empowers those who serve in this role. The Epistle to the Hebrews makes this clear: "And no man takes this honor to himself, but he who is called by God, just as Aaron was" (Hebrews 5:4). This passage emphasizes that the priesthood is not something one can assume by personal choice; it is a role appointed by God, highlighting its heavenly origin.

Similarly, Jesus, the High Priest of the New Covenant, instituted the priestly ministry, saying to His disciples, "As the Father has sent Me, I also send you… Receive the Holy Spirit." (John 20:21-22). By breathing the Holy Spirit upon His apostles, Christ established a ministry that is guided and empowered by the Holy Spirit, affirming that this calling is divinely instituted.

Furthermore, the Acts of the Apostles underscores this divine origin by stating, "Therefore take heed to yourselves and to all the flock, among which the Holy Spirit has made you overseers, to shepherd the church of God which He purchased with His own blood" (Acts 20:28). Here, the role of church leaders is portrayed as an appointment made by the Holy Spirit, reaffirming that the priestly office is not founded on human authority but on God's eternal design. The writer of Hebrews also emphasizes the heavenly nature of the priesthood by pointing to Christ's eternal role: "But Christ came as High Priest of the good things to come, with the greater and more perfect tabernacle not made with hands, that is, not of this creation" (Hebrews 9:11).

This calling transcends time and space, for the priest's ministry is grounded in Christ's eternal priesthood. As the Epistle to the Hebrews teaches, "Seeing then that we have a great High Priest who has passed through the heavens, Jesus the Son of God, let us hold fast our confession" (Hebrews 4:14).

In this way, priests are called to share in Christ's priestly ministry, offering prayers and sacrifices not merely as earthly rituals but as a participation in the heavenly worship that is always ongoing before the throne of God. Every time the priest stands at the altar, he is not simply conducting a liturgical duty; he is entering into the eternal liturgy of heaven, where Christ, the eternal High Priest, continually intercedes for humanity.

In addition, Paul writes to the Ephesians, "And He Himself gave some to be apostles, some prophets, some evangelists, and some pastors and teachers, for the equipping of the saints for the work of ministry, for the edifying of the body of Christ" (Ephesians 4:11-12). This indicates that it is God Himself who assigns different roles within the Church, including the priesthood, for the purpose of sanctifying and building up His people. As Paul further declares, "For we are God's fellow workers; you are God's field, you are God's building" (1 Corinthians 3:9), it is evident that those who serve in the ministry do so as participants in God's divine plan, reflecting a heavenly design rather than a human endeavor.

St. John Chrysostom eloquently captured this divine origin when he wrote:

> "The priesthood is indeed administered on earth, but it ranks among heavenly ordinances, and very rightly so. For it was neither man nor angel, nor archangel, nor any other created power, but the Paraclete Himself, who instituted this calling" (On the Priesthood, Book III).

His words remind us that the priesthood is not a mere earthly institution; it is deeply embedded in God's eternal purpose, and priests are His chosen instruments for the sanctification of the world. Priests share in the eternal priesthood of Christ, participating in a divine ministry that transcends the boundaries of time and space, drawing the faithful into the everlasting worship of God.

## God's Calling

The sacred office of priesthood is not something a person can claim or attain through personal ambition. As Hebrews 5:4 emphasizes, "And no man takes this honor to himself, but he who is called by God, just as Aaron was." This verse underscores that the priesthood is a divine appointment, a sacred calling that originates from God's will. Just as God chose Aaron to serve as a priest, so too must every priest be called by God. The priesthood is not a human institution but a heavenly ordination, and God Himself sets apart those who serve in this sacred role.

Throughout Scripture, we see that it is always God who initiates the call to the priesthood. In the Old Testament, Aaron and his sons were chosen by God Himself to serve as priests, and this calling was confirmed through divine instruction: "You shall anoint them, as you anointed their father, that they may minister to Me as priests; for their anointing shall surely be an everlasting priesthood throughout their generations" (Exodus

40:15). This anointing was not based on merit but on God's sovereign choice, underscoring the truth that no one can assume this role unless called by God.

Similarly, in the New Testament, Jesus made it clear that He did not appoint Himself as High Priest, but rather the Father chose Him. The writer of Hebrews affirms this: "So also Christ did not glorify Himself to become High Priest, but it was He who said to Him: 'You are My Son, Today I have begotten You'" (Hebrews 5:5). This demonstrates that just as the Father called Christ, so every priest is called by God to share in this ministry. It is a calling that involves a profound sense of responsibility, humility, and service, recognizing that it is God who bestows this honor, not human merit.

The consistent message across the Scriptures is that the priesthood originates from God's sovereign will. Those called to this role are chosen not because of their own worthiness but because of God's divine purpose. The sacred nature of this calling demands a response of deep humility and dedication, acknowledging that God sets apart every priest to reflect His love and holiness, just as Christ, the eternal High Priest, was chosen to fulfill the divine plan of salvation.

## Called to Reflect the Eternal High Priest

The New Testament priesthood is intimately connected to Christ's own priesthood. The priest, in every aspect of his ministry, is called to reflect the image of Christ, the High Priest who offered Himself as the perfect sacrifice for the salvation of humanity. The priest does not simply perform religious duties; he is called to embody Christ's sacrificial love and to be a living witness to the mystery of redemption.

In the Old Testament, priests were responsible for offering sacrifices on behalf of the people. In the New Testament, this role is fulfilled in a greater and more profound way through Christ's sacrifice. As the writer of Hebrews explains, "For every high priest is appointed to offer both gifts and sacrifices. Therefore, it is necessary that this One also have something to offer" (Hebrews 8:3). The priesthood today continues this heavenly ministry, grounded in Christ's eternal intercession and sacrifice. The priest does not offer new sacrifices but makes present the one eternal sacrifice of Christ through the celebration of the Eucharist.

## The Priest's Identity: A Heavenly and Earthly Role

The priest's identity is uniquely rooted in both the heavenly and earthly realms. On the one hand, he is called to serve the people of God in their spiritual and sacramental needs. On the other hand, he represents Christ and serves as an intercessor between heaven and earth.

For this dual nature of the priesthood, St. Gregory of Nazianzus wrote,

> "We must begin by purifying ourselves before purifying others; we must be instructed in wisdom before we can instruct others; we must become light, then enlighten; draw close to God, then bring others to Him" (*Oration 2, On the Priesthood*).

The priest's life is thus a constant call to holiness and spiritual growth. Before he can lead others to God, he must draw near to God himself. As Christ said, "Therefore you shall be perfect, just as your Father in heaven is perfect" (Matthew 5:48). The priest must strive for this perfection, not as a lofty goal unattainable by human effort, but as a life-long journey in which God's grace transforms him into a living reflection of Christ's holiness. His identity is shaped not only by external actions but also by his personal union with God.

# The Sacred Responsibility to Serve and Sanctify

The priest's calling is one of service, deeply rooted in the example of Christ, who said, "The Son of Man did not come to be served, but to serve, and to give His life a ransom for many" (Matthew 20:28). In the same way, the priest's ministry is not about personal gain or status; it is about laying down his life in service to others. His authority is not one of domination but of sacrificial leadership, modeled after Christ's own humility and love.

St. John Chrysostom further emphasized this when he said,

> "For the priestly office is indeed discharged on earth, but it is ranked among heavenly ordinances... For neither man, nor angel, nor archangel, nor any other created power, but the Paraclete Himself, instituted this office" (*On the Priesthood, Book III*).

This high calling requires the priest to continually sanctify himself through prayer, fasting, and spiritual discipline so that he may serve as a pure vessel of God's grace.

The priest is not only called to serve but also to sanctify. Through the sacraments, he brings the grace of God to His people, acting as a channel through which divine life flows into the hearts of the faithful. In the liturgy of St. Cyril of Alexandria, the priest prays,

> "O Master, Lord, the Father of mercies... You have made us worthy to stand in this holy place, to serve as priests of Your altar, and to be the ministers of Your holy mysteries."

The priest stands at the altar as an intercessor, offering the prayers of the people to God and bringing down the blessings of heaven upon them.

# The Priest's Participation in the Heavenly Ministry

The priest's role extends beyond the earthly realm. In the celebration of the liturgy, the priest leads the faithful into the eternal worship of heaven. St. John Chrysostom reminds us of the profound mystery of this ministry:

> "When you behold the Lord sacrificed and laid upon the altar, and the priest standing and praying over the Sacrifice... do you then imagine that you are still among men, and standing upon the earth? Are you not, on the contrary, immediately transported to heaven?" (*On the Priesthood, Book III*).

In the Eucharistic celebration, the priest makes present the eternal sacrifice of Christ, which the Holy Spirit accomplishes. Every time the priest celebrates the Eucharist, heaven and earth meet as the faithful partake in the body and blood of Christ. This is not merely a remembrance of a past event, but a genuine participation in the ongoing heavenly liturgy. The priest, as a servant of the sacraments, leads the faithful into this divine mystery, bringing them into communion with the living God.

# Conclusion

The call to the priesthood is a profound mystery and a great responsibility. The priest is not only a shepherd and teacher, but also a shepherd of souls, entrusted with the sacred task of guiding God's people toward holiness and eternal life. His role is both earthly and heavenly, for he stands as a bridge between God and His people, offering the prayers and sacrifices of the Church to the Lord.

As St. Basil's Divine Liturgy reminds us, the priest is called to serve with the angels and archangels, offering worship to God that transcends earthly realities. His identity is deeply rooted in holiness, humility, and self-sacrificial love, for he is called to mirror the ministry of Christ, the angels, and the saints. In accepting this sacred call, the priest embraces a life of profound service, sacrifice, and sanctity. He becomes a vessel of God's grace, a channel through which the divine touches the earthly, and a living reflection of Christ, the eternal High Priest.

# Chapter 2

## The Priest: A Living Reflection of Christ

The priest's calling is more than just a role as a minister of sacraments or a teacher of the faith; it is to embody Christ-like character in every aspect of life. As a shepherd of souls, the priest is called to reflect the virtues of Christ—love, humility, patience, holiness, and self-sacrifice. His heart must be formed in the likeness of Christ, serving as the foundation of his pastoral ministry and making him a living witness to the transformative power of the Gospel.

As St. John Chrysostom once said,

> "The priestly office is full of difficulties and ordeals, and a man must be far removed from all human weaknesses to be able to sustain its burdens" (*On the Priesthood, Book III*).

The priest is called to rise to this high calling, not only through knowledge and skill but through deep moral and spiritual character rooted in Christ's love and virtue.

## Humility: The Foundation of Christ-like Service

At the heart of the priest's Christ-like character is humility. Jesus, the Good Shepherd, exemplified this in His earthly ministry, serving His disciples in humility and love. The priest, like Christ, is called to lead by serving, recognizing that his authority is not for his own advancement but for the sake of those entrusted to his care.

St. Gregory of Nazianzus reminded priests of this sacred responsibility:

> "We must begin by purifying ourselves before purifying others; we must be instructed in wisdom before we can instruct others" (*Oration 2, On the Priesthood*).

The priest's humility before God allows him to serve with a sincere heart, dependent on God's grace rather than his own merit.

The priest is called to be continually reminded that his worthiness comes not from personal accomplishments but from God's grace, as reflected in the prayers of St. Basil's Divine Liturgy:

> "You, O Lord, have called us, though unworthy, to stand before Your holy altar… Grant that we may serve You in humility and with pure hearts."

## Compassion and Gentleness: Shepherding with the Heart of Christ

Along with humility, the priest is called to embody Christ's compassion and gentleness. Just as Christ sought the lost and broken, the priest is called to tend to the needs of his flock with the same tenderness. Jesus said, "Come to Me, all you who labor and are heavy laden, and I will give you rest" (Matthew 11:28). The priest's role as a shepherd is to provide this rest, guiding the faithful with patience and love, bringing them to the healing grace of Christ.

St. Ambrose of Milan emphasized the need for gentleness in the priest's ministry:

> "The servant of the Lord must not quarrel; he must be kind towards all… patient when wronged, gentle, and able to correct opponents with meekness" (*On the Duties of the Clergy, Book II*).

Compassionate leadership requires the priest to be attentive to the struggles of his people, offering them the hope of Christ's mercy and forgiveness.

## Sacrificial Love: The Heart of the Shepherd

Christ, the Good Shepherd, laid down His life for His sheep. This sacrificial love is the model for the priest's ministry. The priest, following Christ's example, must be willing to lay aside personal ambitions and desires, fully dedicating himself to the care of his flock. St. Augustine wrote,

> "The shepherds of Christ's flock ought to imitate the example of Christ, the Good Shepherd, who laid down His life for His sheep" (*Sermon on Pastors*).

In the liturgy of St. Basil, the priest's prayers of intercession for his people reflect this sacrificial love:

> "Remember, O Lord, those who are sick. Heal them according to Your loving-kindness. Remember, O Lord, those who need Your mercy. Comfort them in Your compassion."

The priest is called to lead with the same sacrificial love that Christ demonstrated, offering his life in service to the Church.

## Strength and Endurance in Ministry

The priest's life of service is not without its challenges. Just as Christ endured suffering and opposition for the sake of His mission, the priest is also called to demonstrate patience and perseverance. St. Paul's exhortation to Timothy serves as a reminder: "Preach the word! Be ready in season and out of season. Convince, rebuke, exhort, with all longsuffering and teaching" (2 Timothy 4:2).

> St. John Chrysostom underscored the need for patience in ministry: "For if the priest is called to be

adorned with much discretion and wisdom, there is yet greater need of mildness and great kindness" (*On the Priesthood, Book VI*).

The priest's ability to patiently bear the burdens of ministry, even through difficult circumstances, reflects his deep reliance on God's strength.

## The Priest as a Reflection of Christ's Love

At the center of the priest's ministry is love—sacrificial, unconditional, and selfless love, modeled after Christ's. As Jesus commanded His disciples to "love one another as I have loved you" (John 15:12), the priest is called to embody this divine love in his interactions with others. His service, whether through administering sacraments, offering pastoral care, or preaching the Word, is always to reflect Christ's love for His people.

In the Liturgy of St. Cyril, the priest prays:

> "O Master, Lord, the Father of mercies… we give thanks to You, who have made us worthy to stand in this holy place, to serve as priests of Your altar."

This prayer highlights the priest's identity as one who serves in the image of Christ, offering love and care to the people of God.

## Conclusion

The priest is called to model his life after Christ, the Good Shepherd. Just as Christ leads, protects, and sacrifices for His people, so too must the priest dedicate his life to the care of souls. His ministry is marked by humility, compassion, endurance, and selfless love. By reflecting the heart of Christ, the priest becomes a living icon of God's love, a true shepherd who guides his flock toward eternal life.

# Chapter 3

# Prayer in the Priest's Life

The priest's life is deeply rooted in prayer. His ministry, service, and spiritual leadership depend on his ongoing communion with God through prayer. Just as Christ frequently withdrew to pray and seek the Father's will (Luke 5:16), so too must the priest cultivate a life of intimate fellowship with God. Prayer is not simply an obligation for the priest but a lifeline, a wellspring of divine grace and strength that sustains his soul and empowers him to serve. This chapter explores the centrality of prayer in the priest's life, the different dimensions of priestly prayer, and how this communion with God reflects the love and care of God the Father as revealed in Christ.

## The Necessity of Prayer in the Priest's Life

For the priest, prayer is not an optional or secondary activity; it is the lifeblood of his spiritual and pastoral work. Without a deep, personal relationship with God through prayer, the priest cannot effectively carry out his ministry or guide others in their spiritual journey. His strength, wisdom, and grace come from God alone, and these are accessed and renewed through prayer.

St. John Chrysostom emphasized the absolute necessity of prayer in the priest's life:

> "A priest is called to be fortified by prayer, for it is through prayer that he gains the strength to fulfill the weighty responsibilities of his office. Without prayer, his ministry will become dry, and he will lose the strength to bear the burdens of the people" (*On the Priesthood, Book IV*).

St. Chrysostom's words remind us that the priest's power and effectiveness come not from human effort but through divine communion.

Jesus Himself modeled the necessity of prayer throughout His ministry. The Gospels frequently mention how Jesus would withdraw to solitary places to pray, often before significant events or decisions (Luke 6:12; Matthew 14:23). For the priest, this example serves as a reminder that even amid the demands of ministry, time spent with God in prayer is essential to staying rooted in His will.

St. Paul encourages believers to "pray without ceasing" (1 Thessalonians 5:17), a call that applies especially to priests. The priest's life should be one of constant prayer, not only during formal times of worship or liturgy but throughout every moment of the day. Whether in moments of solitude, pastoral care, or celebrating the sacraments, the priest's heart should always be attuned to God, seeking His guidance, presence, and strength.

# Personal Prayer: The Foundation of the Priest's Spiritual Life

Personal prayer is the foundation of the priest's spiritual life. In this private communion with God, the priest finds rest, renewal, and the strength to serve. Personal prayer enables the priest to pour out their heart before God, to listen for God's voice, and to deepen their intimacy with Him. Without this time of personal devotion, the priest risks becoming spiritually depleted and disconnected from the source of his ministry.

St. Gregory of Nazianzus spoke of the priest's need for personal prayer:

> "The priest who neglects his own prayer life cannot hope to lead others into the presence of God. His strength and wisdom come through his communion

with God, and without this foundation, his ministry becomes hollow" *(Oration 2, On the Priesthood).*

St. Gregory's words highlight the importance of personal devotion as the wellspring of the priest's spiritual vitality.

The priest's personal prayer life should encompass various forms of prayer, including adoration, confession, thanksgiving, and supplication. Each of these forms allows the priest to approach God in different ways, expressing his love, repentance, gratitude, and dependence on God. In particular, the priest should spend time in adoration, worshiping God for who He is and cultivating a heart of reverence and love.

Personal prayer also includes meditation on Scripture. As a man of the Word, the priest should immerse himself in the Scriptures, allowing God to speak to him through the living Word. St. Basil, in his Divine Liturgy, prays:

> "Grant that we may learn the ways of Your commandments and walk in Your truth, that our hearts may be enlightened and our souls filled with Your wisdom."

This prayer reflects the priest's need to be grounded in Scripture, allowing it to shape his heart and guide his ministry.

Psalm 1:2 reminds us of the importance of meditating on God's Word: "But his delight is in the law of the Lord, And in His law he meditates day and night." The priest, through personal prayer and reflection on Scripture, draws closer to God and aligns his heart with the will of the Father.

## Liturgical Prayer: Leading the People of God

In addition to personal prayer, the priest's life is shaped by liturgical prayer—the formal prayers of the Church, particularly the Divine Liturgy and the Liturgy of the Hours. As a leader of worship, the priest stands at the heart of the Church's communal prayer life, guiding the people in offering worship to God.

St. John Chrysostom described the sacredness of liturgical prayer:

> "When the priest stands at the altar, he is not alone, for he is surrounded by angels and the saints who join him in offering worship to God. His role is to lead the people into this heavenly worship, where earth meets heaven and time touches eternity." (*Homilies on the Gospel of Matthew*).

Liturgical prayer unites the Church on earth with the Church in heaven, making the priest's leadership in worship a profound privilege and responsibility.

In leading the people in liturgical prayer, the priest reflects the Father's care for His children, gathering them into the divine presence and offering their prayers to God. The Divine Liturgy of St. Basil expresses this same truth:

> "We thank You, O Lord, for allowing us to stand before You and offer this worship, which is an offering of praise both on earth and in heaven."

The priest's role in liturgical prayer is to lead the people into this eternal praise, where they encounter the presence of God and are drawn closer to the mystery of Christ's love.

## Intercessory Prayer: A Ministry of Compassion

Intercessory prayer is another vital aspect of the priest's life. As a spiritual shepherd, the priest is called to pray for the needs of his flock, lifting up their burdens, struggles, and petitions before God. This ministry of intercession reflects the priest's pastoral heart and his role as a mediator between God and the people, mirroring the love and care of the Father for His children.

St. Gregory the Great emphasized the priest's duty of intercession:

> "The priest stands before God as an intercessor for his people, praying for their needs, their sufferings, and their salvation. His prayer is a shield and a protection for the flock entrusted to his care" (*Pastoral Rule*).

St. Gregory's words highlight the profound responsibility of the priest to bear the burdens of his people in prayer, offering them up to God in love and compassion.

St. Paul's letters are filled with examples of intercessory prayer, as he constantly prayed for the churches he served: "We give thanks to the God and Father of our Lord Jesus Christ, always praying for you" (Colossians 1:3). In the same way, the priest should regularly pray for the members of his parish, asking God to bless, guide, and protect them.

The priest's ministry of intercession reflects Christ's own intercessory role. As the letter to the Hebrews says, "He always lives to make intercession for them" (Hebrews 7:25). The priest, following Christ's example, stands before God on behalf of the people, pleading for their needs and seeking God's grace and mercy for them.

# Contemplative Prayer: Seeking Union with God

Contemplative prayer is the highest form of prayer, in which the soul seeks direct communion with God. This form of prayer transcends words and petitions, resting in the presence of God and allowing His love to fill and transform the heart. For the priest, contemplative prayer is a vital means of deepening his relationship with God and experiencing the fullness of divine love.

St. Gregory of Nazianzus wrote of the importance of contemplation in the life of the priest:

> "The priest is called to seek solitude and silence, where he may encounter God in the depths of his soul. It is in this stillness that the priest finds rest and renewal, drawing strength from the presence of the Almighty." (*Oration 2, On the Priesthood*).

Contemplative prayer allows the priest to enter into the mystery of God's love, which sustains him through the demands of ministry.

In contemplative prayer, the priest experiences the peace that only God can give, a peace that sustains him through the challenges of his ministry. This time of quiet communion with God also helps the priest to discern God's will more clearly, enabling him to lead the people with wisdom and insight. As Psalm 46:10 exhorts, "Be still, and know that I am God," the priest finds strength and direction in the stillness of contemplative prayer.

## The Priest's Prayer Life and His Ministry

The priest's prayer life is the foundation of his entire ministry. Without a strong and consistent prayer life, the priest cannot effectively serve the people of God. His ability to teach, preach, counsel, and lead is directly tied to his communion with God through prayer. As the priest deepens his relationship with God, his ministry becomes more fruitful, filled with the grace and power that come from the Holy Spirit.

St. John Chrysostom emphasized the relationship between prayer and ministry:

> "A priest who does not pray cannot hope to fulfill his ministry. His strength comes from his communion with God, and it is through prayer that he receives

the grace to teach, to counsel, and to guide." (*On the Priesthood, Book V*).

St. Chrysostom's words remind us that the priest's effectiveness is directly tied to his devotion to prayer.

In the Divine Liturgy of St. Basil, the priest prays:

> "Grant, O Lord, that I may always remain in Your presence, drawing strength and wisdom from Your love, so that I may lead Your people with a heart full of grace and truth."

This prayer reflects the priest's dependence on God for the strength to carry out his ministry. Through prayer, the priest continually receives the grace to reflect the love and care of God the Father, leading his people with compassion and wisdom.

## Conclusion

Prayer is the foundation of the priest's life and ministry. Through personal prayer, liturgical prayer, intercession, and contemplation, the priest remains in constant communion with God, drawing strength and wisdom from the divine source. This ongoing relationship with God sustains the priest's spiritual life, empowers his ministry, and enables him to lead the people of God with love and grace. A life of prayer is not only essential for the priest's own spiritual growth but also for the spiritual well-being of the entire congregation he serves.

# Chapter 4

# The Priest's Call to Holiness

The priest is not merely a religious figure or administrator; he is a man consecrated to God, called to live a life of holiness and purity in imitation of Christ. This call to holiness is not only for his personal sanctification, but also for the sanctification of the people of God, as the priest's holiness has a profound impact on those he serves. His life must be a living testimony of God's presence, embodying the divine holiness that he proclaims and imparts to the faithful. In the words of Scripture, the priest is called to be holy as God is holy: "You shall be holy, for I the Lord your God am holy" (Leviticus 19:2).

St. John Chrysostom beautifully expressed the high calling of the priesthood:

> "A priest ought to be as pure as if he were standing in heaven itself, in the midst of those angelic powers. He ought to be as holy as the angels, for his work is greater than that of the angels. They are sent to minister to souls, but the priest brings down the Holy Spirit upon the altar" (*On the Priesthood, Book III*).

St. Chrysostom's words underscore the immense responsibility and sanctity required of the priest, who must live a life worthy of the sacred mysteries he celebrates.

## The Priest as a Model of Holiness

As a shepherd of souls, the priest is called to be a visible model of holiness for the people of God. His actions and words must reflect the Gospel he proclaims, for the faithful look to him as an example of how to live a life pleasing to God. This makes the priest's personal holiness not just a private matter but an essential aspect of his ministry. His life becomes a living testimony that inspires others to seek God.

St. Gregory of Nazianzus stressed this responsibility:

> "We must begin by purifying ourselves before purifying others; we must become light, then enlighten; draw close to God, then bring others to Him; be sanctified, then sanctify" (*Oration 2, On the Priesthood*).

St. Gregory's words reflect the deep truth that the priest is called to first strive for holiness himself before leading others. His spiritual life is essential for his ministry, and without it, he cannot effectively guide the faithful toward God.

The Divine Liturgy of St. Basil offers a profound prayer for this grace:

> "O Lord, purify my heart, that I may offer You this sacrifice without blemish, and that I may lead Your people in the way of holiness. Grant that my life may be a reflection of Your holiness, that I may guide others by the example of my faith."

This prayer highlights the priest's desire to be a model of holiness, recognizing that his own sanctity is crucial in leading others toward a deeper relationship with God.

## The Sacrificial Life of the Priest

The priest's call to holiness is deeply intertwined with the call to a life of sacrifice. Just as Christ offered His life for the salvation of humanity, the priest is called to offer his life for the Church. This sacrificial dimension is central to the priesthood, requiring the priest to lay down his personal desires, ambitions, and comforts for the sake of his flock.

St. Paul's exhortation to the Romans speaks directly to this call: "I beseech you therefore, brethren, by the mercies of God, that you present your bodies a living sacrifice, holy, acceptable to God, which is your reasonable service" (Romans 12:1). The priest's entire life is meant to be an ongoing offering to God, reflecting the self-giving love of Christ, who came to serve rather than to be served (Mark 10:45).

St. Gregory the Great reflected on this sacrificial aspect:

> "The priest is called to not think of himself but of his people. His life is no longer his own; it belongs to God and the Church. In offering the sacrifice of the Mass, the priest is called to offer himself as well, uniting his own sacrifices to the sacrifice of Christ" (*Pastoral Rule*).

This understanding of the priesthood as a life of self-giving mirrors Christ's own sacrifice, calling the priest to follow the same path of love and service.

In the Divine Liturgy of St. Cyril of Alexandria, the priest prays:

> "Grant, O Lord, that I may offer my life as a living sacrifice, holy and acceptable to You. Help me to lay aside my own desires, that I may serve You and Your people with a heart full of love and humility."

This prayer captures the essence of the priest's ministry, recognizing that his life is to be offered fully to God and His people.

## A Life of Prayer and Communion with God

At the heart of the priest's call to holiness is his life of prayer. The priest's ministry flows from his communion with God, and it is through prayer that this communion is deepened. Prayer is not simply a duty for the priest; it is the lifeblood of his spiritual life, the source of his strength, and the wellspring from which his ministry flows. Without a strong prayer life, the priest risks becoming disconnected from the grace of God that sustains his vocation.

St. John Chrysostom emphasized the centrality of prayer in the priest's life:

> "The priest is called to be a man of prayer, for it is through prayer that he draws down the grace of God to sanctify his own soul and to bless the people. Without prayer, the priest's ministry becomes a lifeless formality, devoid of the power of the Holy Spirit" (*On the Priesthood, Book IV*).

Prayer is the priest's link to divine grace, enabling him to fulfill his sacred duties with the power of the Holy Spirit.

The Divine Liturgy of St. Basil includes a prayer for the grace of constant prayer:

> "Grant, O Lord, that I may always remain in Your presence, offering You the sacrifice of praise with a heart full of love. Help me to pray without ceasing, that I may be strengthened by Your grace and live a life worthy of the calling I have received."

This prayer reflects the priest's need for continuous communion with God, recognizing that his ability to serve is rooted in his life of prayer.

## The Priest as a Witness to Holiness

The priest's holiness is not only for his own benefit but also for the sanctification of those he serves. As a witness to God's holiness, the priest's life becomes a beacon of light in a world marked by sin and darkness. His holiness has a transformative effect on the faithful, drawing them closer to God and inspiring them to seek holiness in their own lives.

St. Gregory of Nazianzus spoke of the priest's witness:

> "The priest is called to be like a city set on a hill, whose light cannot be hidden. His life must shine with the holiness of God, drawing others to the truth of the Gospel. For the priest's holiness is not for his own glory but for the glory of God and the salvation of souls" (*Oration 2, On the Priesthood*).

St. Gregory's words remind us that the priest's life of holiness serves as a powerful witness to the world, leading others toward the truth and love of God.

The Divine Liturgy of St. Cyril includes a prayer for this witness:

> "O Lord may my life be a reflection of Your holiness, that I may lead Your people by the example of my faith. Help me to walk in the light of Your truth, that others may see Your glory and be drawn to Your love."

This prayer expresses the priest's desire to be a faithful witness to God's holiness, guiding others by the light of Christ.

# The Priest's Holiness and the Sanctification of the People

The holiness of the priest is intimately connected to the sanctification of the people. When a priest lives a life of holiness, he becomes an instrument of God's grace, helping the faithful deepen their relationship with God. His personal holiness strengthens the power of his ministry, enabling him to lead others toward spiritual growth and sanctification effectively.

St. John Chrysostom emphasized this connection:

> "When the priest is holy, the people are sanctified. For the priest is the one who offers the holy sacrifice,

who prays for the people, who blesses them in the name of the Lord. His holiness, therefore, is essential for the sanctification of the Church" (*On the Priesthood, Book VI*).

St. Chrysostom's words highlight the vital role that the priest's holiness plays in the spiritual life of the Church. The priest, through his sanctity, serves as a channel of God's grace to the people.

The Divine Liturgy of St. Basil includes a prayer for the sanctification of the people:

> "Sanctify Your people, O Lord, through the prayers of Your priest. Grant that they may grow in holiness and be strengthened by Your grace, that they may walk in the way of righteousness and inherit the kingdom of heaven."

This prayer reflects the priest's role as an intercessor whose holiness and prayers contribute to the sanctification of the faithful.

## Conclusion

The priest's call to holiness is crucial for the entirety of his ministry. He is a man set apart for God, called to live a life of purity, sacrifice, and prayer in imitation of Christ. His personal holiness is not only for his own spiritual benefit but also for the sanctification of the Church. As a witness to God's holiness, the priest's life becomes a reflection of the divine love and grace that he is called to impart to the people of God.

St. John Chrysostom's words continue to inspire priests today:

> "A priest ought to be as pure as if he is standing in heaven itself, in the midst of those angelic powers."

Through his life of holiness, the priest fulfills his sacred calling, leading the faithful toward the fullness of life in Christ. As a man consecrated to God, the priest becomes a beacon of light in a darkened world, guiding souls toward the love and truth of God and reflecting the holiness of the One who has called him.

# Chapter 5

## The Priest as a Spiritual Father

The priest is called to be more than just a shepherd or administrator in the Church; he is called to be a spiritual father, nurturing the souls entrusted to him with the same care and attention that a father gives to his children. This role as a spiritual father requires the priest to guide, instruct, and encourage the faithful, helping them grow in their relationship with God and mature in their spiritual life. The priest's paternal care reflects the heavenly Father's love, and through his ministry, he helps the faithful experience the tenderness, guidance, and correction that lead them toward holiness.

St. John Chrysostom beautifully described the priest's fatherly role:

> "The priest is a father to all his people, caring for them with a love that surpasses the love of earthly fathers. For his concern is not for their physical needs, but for the salvation of their souls. He must labor with them, weep with them, and rejoice with them, just as a father does with his children" (*On the Priesthood, Book III*).

St. Chrysostom's words remind us that the priest's love for his people is spiritual, focused on their eternal well-being, and expressed through his daily care and guidance.

## The Priest as a Guide in the Spiritual Life

As a spiritual father, the priest plays a central role in guiding the faithful in their spiritual journey. This involves providing instruction in the faith, offering counsel in times of difficulty, and helping the faithful discern God's will for their lives. The priest's guidance is not merely intellectual but deeply spiritual, rooted in prayer and the wisdom that comes from a life lived in communion with God. The priest's ability to guide others on the path of holiness depends on his closeness to God and commitment to living a life of virtue.

St. Gregory of Nazianzus emphasized the importance of the priest's spiritual maturity in guiding others:

> "We must begin by purifying ourselves before purifying others; we must be instructed in wisdom before we can instruct others; we must become light, then enlighten; draw close to God, then bring others to Him" (*Oration 2, On the Priesthood*).

St. Gregory's words remind us that the priest cannot guide others to God unless he himself is striving for holiness. His life must reflect the virtues he seeks to cultivate in his people, and his wisdom must flow from his own intimate relationship with God.

In the Divine Liturgy of St. Basil, the priest prays for wisdom to guide the faithful:

> "Grant, O Lord, that Your servant may lead Your people with wisdom and discernment. Fill him with the knowledge of Your will, that he may offer wise counsel to those who seek his guidance and help them to walk in the path of holiness."

This prayer reflects the priest's dependence on God's grace to fulfill his role as a spiritual guide, recognizing that true wisdom comes from God and is necessary for leading others on the journey of faith.

## Nurturing the Souls of the Faithful

A spiritual father's role is not only to guide but also to nurture the spiritual growth of his children in the faith. Just as a father provides for the physical and emotional needs of his children, the priest is called to provide for the spiritual needs of his people. This includes teaching them how to pray, helping them understand the Scriptures, and encouraging them to participate in the sacraments. The priest's nurturing care helps the faithful grow in their relationship with God, deepening their faith and leading them toward greater holiness.

St. John Chrysostom likened the priest's role to that of a gardener:

> "The priest is like a gardener, whose task is to cultivate the souls of the faithful, nurturing them with the Word of God, watering them with the sacraments, and pruning them with correction, so that they may bear fruit in holiness" (*Homilies on Matthew*).

St. Chrysostom's metaphor emphasizes the priest's responsibility to care for the spiritual growth of his people, patiently guiding them toward maturity in the faith.

In the Divine Liturgy of St. Cyril of Alexandria, the priest prays for the grace to nurture the faithful:

> "We thank You, O Lord, for making us worthy to stand before You and to serve as ministers of Your holy mysteries. Grant that we may nurture the souls entrusted to us with love and care, guiding them in the way of truth and helping them grow in Your grace."

This prayer reflects the priest's role as a spiritual nurturer, entrusted with the care of souls and responsible for helping them grow in the knowledge and love of God.

## Encouraging Spiritual Maturity

One of the key tasks of a spiritual father is to encourage the faithful to grow in spiritual maturity, helping them move beyond a superficial understanding of the faith to a deep and abiding relationship with God. The priest is called to challenge his people to live lives of virtue, deepen their prayer life, and seek holiness in all areas of their lives. This requires the priest to be both gentle and firm, offering encouragement and correction as needed to help the faithful grow in their spiritual lives.

St. Paul's words to the Corinthians highlight this need for spiritual maturity: "And I, brethren, could not speak to you as to spiritual people but as to carnal, as to babes in Christ. I fed you with milk and not with solid food; for until now you were not able to receive it, and even now you are still not able" (1 Corinthians 3:1-2). The priest, as a spiritual father, must help his people progress from spiritual infancy to maturity, guiding them through the various stages of spiritual growth and fostering a deeper understanding of the faith.

St. Gregory the Great spoke of the priest's role in encouraging spiritual maturity:

> "The priest is called not to be content with simply providing for the spiritual needs of his people. He must challenge them to grow, to seek holiness, and to strive for perfection. For the priest's task is not only to feed the lambs but to lead them to green pastures, where they may grow strong in the Lord" (*Pastoral Rule*).

St. Gregory's words remind us that the priest's role is not only to provide spiritual nourishment but also to encourage the faithful to seek greater holiness and spiritual growth.

In the Divine Liturgy of St. Basil, the priest prays for the spiritual growth of his people:

> "O Lord, strengthen the faith of Your people, that they may grow in love and holiness. Help them to mature in their spiritual lives, that they may be filled

with the knowledge of Your will and walk in a manner worthy of the Gospel."

This prayer reflects the priest's desire to see the faithful grow in their relationship with God, maturing in their faith and living lives that reflect the holiness of Christ.

## Offering Correction with Love

As a spiritual father, the priest is also called to be willing to offer correction when necessary, helping the faithful avoid sin and stay on the path of righteousness. This correction must always be offered with love and compassion, recognizing that the goal is not to condemn but to guide the person back to God. The priest, like a father, must be both firm and gentle, correcting with kindness and leading the faithful toward repentance and conversion.

St. John Chrysostom emphasized the importance of offering correction with love:

> "The priest is called to correct his people not with anger or harshness, but with gentleness and love, for the goal of correction is not to punish but to heal. Just as a father disciplines his children with love, so too the priest is called to guide his people with patience and compassion" (*On the Priesthood, Book VI*).

St. Chrysostom's words remind us that the priest's role in offering correction is rooted in his desire to see the faithful grow in holiness, and his correction must always be motivated by love.

In the Divine Liturgy of St. Basil, the priest prays for the wisdom to offer correction with love:

> "Grant, O Lord, that Your servant may guide Your people with wisdom and love, correcting them when necessary with gentleness and patience, that they

may grow in holiness and walk in the light of Your truth."

This prayer reflects the priest's responsibility to guide the faithful with love, helping them overcome sin and deepen their relationship with God.

## The Joy of Spiritual Fatherhood

Being a spiritual father is not only a responsibility but also a source of great joy for the priest. Just as a father rejoices in the growth and success of his children, the priest finds joy in seeing the spiritual growth of his people. When the faithful grow in holiness, deepen their relationship with God, and live lives that reflect the Gospel, the priest experiences the joy of knowing that his ministry has borne fruit in the lives of those he serves.

St. Paul expressed this joy in his letter to the Thessalonians: "For what is our hope, or joy, or crown of rejoicing? Is it not even you in the presence of our Lord Jesus Christ at His coming? For you are our glory and joy" (1 Thessalonians 2:19-20). The priest, like St. Paul, finds his joy in the spiritual growth of his people, knowing that his ministry has helped them draw closer to God.

St. Gregory of Nazianzus also spoke of the joy of spiritual fatherhood:

> "There is no greater joy for a priest than to see the souls entrusted to him grow in holiness and love for God. For in their growth, the priest finds his own fulfillment, knowing that he has played a part in leading them to the light of Christ" (*Oration 2, On the Priesthood*).

St. Gregory's words remind us that the priest's joy is found in the spiritual success of his people, as their growth in holiness is the fruit of his ministry.

In the Divine Liturgy of St. Cyril of Alexandria, the priest prays for the grace to experience the joy of spiritual fatherhood:

> "We thank You, O Lord, for the joy of seeing Your people grow in faith and holiness. Grant that we may continue to serve them with love and care, guiding them in the way of truth and rejoicing in their growth in Your grace."

This prayer reflects the priest's desire to see his people grow in their relationship with God and the joy he experiences in witnessing their spiritual progress.

## Conclusion

The priest's role as a spiritual father is one of the most important and rewarding aspects of his ministry. As a guide, nurturer, and protector of souls, the priest is called to lead the faithful in their spiritual growth, helping them to deepen their relationship with God and grow in holiness. His fatherly care is a reflection of the love of the heavenly Father, who desires that all His children come to know Him and experience the fullness of life in Christ.

St. John Chrysostom's reflection on spiritual fatherhood captures the heart of the priest's ministry:

> "The priest is a father to all his people, caring for them with a love that surpasses the love of earthly fathers. For his concern is not for their physical needs but for the salvation of their souls."

In every act of spiritual fatherhood, the priest is called to reflect the love of Christ, guiding the faithful with wisdom, patience, and compassion and rejoicing in their growth in the Lord.

# Chapter 6

## The Priest's Pastoral Ministry

Pastoral leadership and service lie at the heart of the priest's calling, reflecting the care, love, and wisdom of God the Father, revealed in Jesus Christ, the Good Shepherd. The priest, as a shepherd of souls, is entrusted with the care of God's people, leading them in faith, protecting them from spiritual harm, and nurturing their relationship with God. His leadership, modeled on Christ, is marked by sacrificial love, humble service, and compassionate care, embodying the virtues that guide pastoral ministry.

The priest's pastoral role extends beyond spiritual leadership to include acts of mercy that demonstrate God's love for those in need. Just as Christ ministered to the sick, cared for the poor, welcomed the outcast, and showed compassion to the marginalized, the priest is called to follow this example. This involves visiting the sick and comforting the dying, offering hope and healing through prayers and sacraments. It includes helping the needy, supporting the poor, and advocating for justice, reflecting Christ's concern for the vulnerable. The priest is also called to welcome strangers, extending hospitality and a sense of belonging. His pastoral ministry also includes visiting those in prison, bringing the light of the Gospel and the assurance of God's forgiveness and grace.

Through these charitable services, the priest embodies the love and compassion of Christ, fulfilling his sacred responsibility to serve as a shepherd who cares for every member of his flock. In each act of service, whether guiding the faithful, supporting the struggling, or comforting the brokenhearted, the priest reflects the heart of the Good Shepherd, who laid down His life for the sheep.

## Shepherding the Flock with Love and Humility

The priest's pastoral role is one of servant-leadership, modeled after Christ, who said, "I am the good shepherd. The good shepherd gives His life for the sheep" (John 10:11). The priest, like Christ, is called to lay down his life in service to his flock, leading them not with worldly authority but with humility, love, and a willingness to sacrifice for their spiritual welfare.

St. Peter's exhortation captures this ideal: "Shepherd the flock of God which is among you, serving as overseers, not by compulsion but willingly, not for dishonest gain but eagerly" (1 Peter 5:2). The priest's leadership is an expression of divine care, guiding the faithful toward holiness, ensuring their spiritual safety, and nurturing their faith journey. As Jesus modeled humble service by washing His disciples' feet (John 13:14), the priest is called to lead through acts of humility, service, and love.

St. Paul also provided a powerful example of pastoral care in his farewell speech to the priests of the church in Ephesus. He said, "You know, from the first day that I came to Asia, in what manner I always lived among you, serving the Lord with all humility, with many tears and trials which happened to me by the plotting of the Jews; how I kept back nothing that was helpful, but proclaimed it to you, and taught you publicly and from house to house" (Acts 20:18-20). St. Paul's words highlight his dedication, humility, and willingness to endure hardships for the sake of his flock.

He further encourages the priests, "Therefore take heed to yourselves and to all the flock, among which the Holy Spirit has made you overseers, to shepherd the church of God which He purchased with His own blood" (Acts 20:28). This emphasizes that the priest's responsibility is a sacred trust, as the flock is precious to God, redeemed by Christ's sacrifice. Just as St. Paul poured himself out in service, the priest is called to shepherd with the same love, vigilance, and dedication, aware that his ministry is not merely a duty but a divine calling to nurture and protect the people of God.

## Serving with Compassion and Grace

The essence of the priest's ministry is to serve with deep compassion, mirroring Christ's love for His people. As a spiritual father, the priest is called to offer mercy, kindness, and understanding, providing comfort to those in need, support to the weak, and healing to the brokenhearted. St. John Chrysostom emphasized this pastoral aspect, stating,

> "The priest is called to be like a father to all, a comforter in sorrow, a protector in danger, and a healer of souls" (*On the Priesthood, Book III*).

Christ's sacrificial care for the lost and suffering serves as the ultimate model of compassion for the priest. As Jesus looked upon the crowds and pitied them, seeing they were "like sheep without a shepherd" (Matthew 9:36), so the priest must have an open heart to the sufferings of his people, providing them with the balm of God's love and mercy. The priest is also called to bind up the brokenhearted, as Christ fulfilled the prophecy of Isaiah: "The Spirit of the Lord God is upon Me Because the Lord has anointed Me To preach good tidings to the poor; He has sent Me to heal the brokenhearted, To proclaim liberty to the captives, And the opening of the prison to those who are bound" (Isaiah 61:1).

## Visiting the Sick and Comforting the Dying

The priest's pastoral ministry involves bringing hope, peace, and healing to those who are ill and facing death. Just as Christ demonstrated compassion by healing the sick and raising the dead (Luke 4:40; John 11:43-44), the priest is called to be a vessel of Christ's presence among those who are suffering. Through prayers, sacraments, and comforting words, the priest provides spiritual solace, reminding the afflicted of God's unending love and care even in times of distress.

St. James emphasizes the role of the priest in ministering to the sick: "Is anyone among you sick? Let him call for the elders of the church, and let them pray over him, anointing him with oil in the name of the Lord." (James 5:14). The act of anointing and prayer is not merely a ritual but a demonstration of God's grace and healing power. In these moments, the priest embodies the compassion of Christ, offering reassurance to those nearing the end of life that they are not alone and that their lives are held in God's hands. This ministry of presence is a profound expression of the love of the Good Shepherd, who cares for every one of His sheep.

## Helping the Needy and Supporting the Poor

Acts of charity and justice are integral to the priest's pastoral ministry, reflecting the heart of Christ, who came to serve and not to be served (Mark 10:45). Throughout His ministry, Jesus demonstrated a deep concern for the poor and the needy, feeding the hungry and defending the vulnerable. The priest is called to emulate this concern, actively helping to meet both the physical and spiritual needs of those in poverty.

Jesus said, "Give to him who asks you, and from him who wants to borrow from you do not turn away" (Matthew 5:42), emphasizing the importance of generosity and compassion. The priest's ministry involves organizing assistance for those in need, whether through food distribution, financial aid, or spiritual support. Moreover, the priest serves as an advocate for justice, speaking up for the oppressed and working towards solutions that address the root causes of poverty and inequality. By serving "the least of these" (Matthew 25:35-40), the priest fulfills Christ's command, ensuring that the church remains a beacon of hope and support for the marginalized.

## Hosting Strangers and Welcoming the Outcast

Hospitality is a significant element of the priest's role, rooted in the biblical tradition of welcoming the stranger. Scripture calls on the faithful to show kindness to those who are new or different, saying, "Do not forget to entertain strangers, for by so doing some have unwittingly entertained angels" (Hebrews 13:2). The priest's ministry of hospitality is an extension of Christ's welcoming embrace, which is evident in His willingness to dine with tax collectors, sinners, and those considered outcasts (Luke 15:1-2).

In this spirit, the priest is called to cultivate a church environment where all feel accepted and valued, offering a safe space where individuals can find spiritual nourishment, friendship, and a sense of community. The priest's welcoming attitude serves as a living testament to God's inclusive love for those who are new to the congregation, refugees, or individuals who feel alienated from society. By offering shelter, guidance, and a listening ear, the priest mirrors Christ's love and acceptance, inviting others to experience the transformative power of God's grace.

## Visiting Those in Prisons

Christ's teaching underscores the importance of visiting those who are imprisoned: "I was in prison, and you came to Me" (Matthew 25:36). The priest's pastoral ministry extends to those who are incarcerated, as they, too, are part of the flock entrusted to his care. Many prisoners face isolation, guilt, and a sense of hopelessness. The priest's visits can bring the light of the Gospel, offering a message of forgiveness, hope, and redemption.

As the author of Hebrews encourages, "Remember the prisoners as if chained with them" (Hebrews 13:3), the priest is encouraged to empathize with and support those behind bars, showing them the path to reconciliation with God. These visits are not just about providing spiritual guidance; they are about affirming the inherent dignity of each person, reminding them that no one is beyond the reach of God's love. By offering a compassionate ear, spiritual counsel, and prayer, the priest helps those in prison to see themselves through God's eyes, as beloved children who are always capable of redemption and renewal.

## Leading with Wisdom and Discernment

To effectively shepherd the flock, the priest must rely on divine wisdom and discernment, which come through prayer and deep communion with God. This wisdom allows him to offer spiritual guidance, correct with patience, and protect his flock from spiritual dangers. As St. Gregory the Great reflected,

> "The care of souls is the art of arts... It requires great compassion, great kindness, and a willingness to bear the burden of others as if it were your own."

The priest's role as a spiritual guide, counselor, and protector is further emphasized by St. John Chrysostom, who compared the priest to a spiritual physician, discerning the right remedy for each soul (*On the Priesthood, Book VI*). Whether providing gentle encouragement, firm correction, or wise counsel, the priest's leadership must reflect Christ's wisdom and care for each individual.

## Bearing the Burdens of the Flock

Pastoral ministry often involves walking with the faithful through their joys and struggles. St. Paul's instruction to "Bear one another's burdens, and so fulfill the law of Christ" (Galatians 6:2) encapsulates the priest's responsibility to share in the sufferings and challenges of his people, providing them with spiritual support and hope.

As St. Gregory the Great emphasized, the priest must not turn away from the sorrows of his flock but instead share in their burdens, offering comfort and consolation in the love of Christ. This compassionate solidarity reflects Christ's own willingness to bear humanity's burdens on the cross.

## Conclusion

The priest's pastoral ministry is both a sacred responsibility and a profound expression of God's fatherly love, revealed in Jesus Christ. As a shepherd of souls, the priest is called to lead with humility, serve with compassion, and protect with vigilance, reflecting the heart of the Good Shepherd. His leadership, modeled on Christ, is a life of self-giving love, guiding the faithful toward holiness and eternal life.

This pastoral calling extends beyond spiritual leadership to encompass practical acts of mercy that bring Christ's love to those in need. The priest cares for the sick and the dying, offering prayers, sacraments, and words of comfort that convey hope and healing. He serves the poor and the needy by organizing assistance and advocating for justice, reflecting Christ's concern for the marginalized. The priest welcomes strangers, extending hospitality and inclusion, and reaches out to those who are isolated, including prisoners, bringing them the light of the Gospel and the assurance of God's forgiveness and grace.

In every act of pastoral care, whether comforting the afflicted, supporting the vulnerable, or guiding the lost, the priest embodies the compassion of Christ, who said, "I was hungry, and you gave Me food; I was thirsty and you gave Me drink; I was a stranger, and you took Me in; I was naked, and you clothed Me; I was sick and you visited Me; I was in prison, and you came to Me" (Matthew 25:35-36).

This sacred ministry requires a profound commitment to the care of souls, embodying the love and grace of Christ in every act of pastoral service. Through his dedication to the sick, the poor, the prisoners, the strangers, and all those in need, the priest fulfills his calling as a servant-shepherd, leading his flock with the love and compassion of the Good Shepherd.

# Chapter 7

# Teaching, Preaching, and Evangelizing

One of the most essential responsibilities of the priest is his role as a teacher and preacher of the Word of God. Entrusted with the divine truth of the Gospel, the priest is called to proclaim it to the faithful, ensuring that the people of God are instructed in the ways of holiness. This sacred duty is more than mere communication; it is an act of evangelization that brings people into deeper communion with God through the transformative power of His Word. The priest's teaching ministry is an extension of Christ's mission, which is to proclaim the good news of salvation to all (Luke 4:18).

The priest's ability to teach and preach the Word is vital to the spiritual vitality of the Church. Without sound teaching, the faithful cannot grow in their knowledge of God, and the Church cannot fulfill its mission in the world.

## The Priest as a Proclaimer of the Word

The priest's role as a teacher begins with his proclamation of the Word of God. Whether from the pulpit, in catechesis, or in personal conversations, the priest is called to announce the Gospel with clarity and conviction. He is a herald of the divine message, entrusted with making known the mysteries of salvation to the people of God. This task requires not only knowledge of the Scriptures but also a deep, personal relationship with the Word of God, which the priest is called to study, meditate on, and live by (Psalm 1:2).

St. Paul highlights the sacredness of this role: "How then shall they call on Him in whom they have not believed? And how shall they believe in Him of whom they have not heard? And how shall they hear without a preacher? ... So, then faith comes by hearing, and hearing by the word of God" (Romans

10:14-17). The priest, as a preacher, facilitates this hearing, delivering the life-giving Word that can transform hearts and bring salvation.

St. Gregory the Theologian emphasized the priest's sacred duty to proclaim the truth:

> "You, O Lord, have given us Your Holy Scriptures for the salvation of our souls. You have commanded us to preach and teach Your Word in all wisdom and understanding so that Your people may grow in the knowledge of the truth" (*Divine Liturgy of St. Gregory*).

This liturgical prayer highlights that the priest is not merely delivering information but speaking the life-giving Word of God, which brings salvation and transformation to those who hear it.

## Preaching with Power and Conviction

Preaching is one of the primary ways in which the priest fulfills his role as a proclaimer of the Word. The homily during the liturgy is not just a moral exhortation but a sacred moment when the Word of God is brought to life for the people of God. Through preaching, the priest helps the faithful understand the Scriptures, apply them to their lives, and grow in their relationship with God.

St. Paul charged Timothy, "Preach the word! Be ready in season and out of season. Convince, rebuke, exhort, with all longsuffering and teaching" (2 Timothy 4:2). This underscores the weight of preaching as the means through which the Word reaches the hearts of the faithful, encouraging them in their spiritual journey.

St. Augustine of Hippo described the power of preaching:

> "The preaching of the Church truly continues without change and is ever the same, as the Spirit of God gives life and vitality to it" (*Against Heresies, Book III*).

St. Augustine's words remind us that the priest's preaching must always be faithful to the Gospel, preserving it from distortion and presenting it as the life-giving treasure that sanctifies the people of God.

In St. Basil's Divine Liturgy, we find a reflection on the power of preaching within the mystery of salvation:

> "You have established this great mystery of salvation for us. You have given us this service of sacrifice and offering, that we may glorify Your holy name and sanctify Your people."

Preaching, therefore, is not merely about delivering a message; it is a sacred act that draws the faithful deeper into communion with God and helps sanctify them through the truth of the Gospel (John 17:17).

Here is the merged heading that combines the key elements of both sections, focusing on the priest's role in both protecting and teaching the flock:

## Teaching Sound Doctrine

A central aspect of the priest's pastoral duty is to instruct the faithful in sound doctrine, ensuring they are well-grounded in the truth of the Gospel. The priest's role as a teacher extends beyond preaching; it involves guiding the faithful in understanding the Church's teachings and passing on the sacred tradition that has been handed down from the apostles. This requires the priest to be knowledgeable in Scripture, theology, and the teachings of the Church Fathers so he can provide clear and accurate instruction. The priest's teaching is not his own; it is the teaching of Christ entrusted to him by the Church to be faithfully transmitted to every generation.

St. Paul exhorted Titus, "But as for you, speak the things which are proper for sound doctrine" (Titus 2:1). The priest's teaching must be rooted in sound doctrine, guided by the Holy Spirit, and marked by wisdom and compassion. As St. John Chrysostom noted,

> "There is a greater need for mildness and great kindness because it is not possible otherwise to rectify the careless and the rebellious souls" (*On the Priesthood, Book VI*).

Through his teaching, the priest helps to deepen the faith of the people, leading them to a clearer understanding of God's will and guiding them toward a life of holiness.

St. Irenaeus of Lyons emphasized the importance of fidelity in teaching:

> "The preaching of the Church truly continues without change... For the Church guards the truth carefully, as a great treasure in an excellent vessel, and this treasure is the Word of God" (*Against Heresies, Book III*).

The priest is called to safeguard this treasure, ensuring that his teaching remains true to the apostolic faith and leads people to salvation. By grounding the faithful in sound doctrine, the priest equips them to discern truth from error, strengthening their faith and enabling them to stand firm in a world of conflicting beliefs.

## Protecting the Flock from False Doctrines

In addition to teaching, the priest's pastoral duty includes safeguarding the spiritual well-being of his flock by protecting them from spiritual harm. Just as a shepherd protects his sheep from predators, the priest is called to guard his people from false teachings, worldly temptations, and spiritual attacks. St. Paul encouraged Timothy to "Guard what was committed to your trust, avoiding the profane and idle babblings and contradictions of what is falsely called 'knowledge'" (1 Timothy 6:20). The priest, likewise, must be vigilant in defending the truth of the Gospel, ensuring that his flock remains safe in the embrace of Christ's truth.

This protective role is echoed in the prayers of the Divine Liturgy, where the priest asks God to preserve the Church from all heresy and false doctrine. Through his vigilance, the priest helps maintain the unity and purity of the Church, standing as a defender of the faith against error and deception. His role involves not only refuting false teachings but also guiding the faithful away from influences that could lead them astray, providing them with the spiritual strength to resist temptation and remain faithful to the Gospel.

By faithfully teaching sound doctrine and guarding the flock against spiritual dangers, the priest fulfills his role as a shepherd who both nurtures and protects his people. His commitment to truth ensures that the faithful are equipped with the knowledge and wisdom needed to follow the path of salvation, growing in their relationship with God and standing firm in the face of trials.

## Evangelizing with Zeal

The priest's teaching and preaching ministry extends to evangelization. He is called to bring the Gospel to the world, sharing the good news of Christ with those who do not yet know Him. St. Paul's passionate declaration captures this call: "Woe to me if I do not preach the gospel!" (1 Corinthians 9:16). The priest, as a representative of the Church, must go beyond the walls of the Church, reaching out to the lost with zeal and urgency.

The Liturgy of St. Cyril of Alexandria offers a prayer that captures the heart of the priest's evangelistic mission:

> "O Master, Lord, the Father of mercies... we give thanks to You... to be ministers of Your holy mysteries, just as You have called us through the voice of Your only begotten Son, our Lord Jesus Christ, who is the Good Shepherd of Your people."

The priest, following Christ's example, must bring others into the flock, sharing the Good News with those outside the Church.

## A Life Rooted in the Word

For the priest to effectively teach, preach, and evangelize, his own life must be rooted in the Word of God. The priest cannot give what he does not have, so he must constantly immerse himself in Scripture, prayer, and study. His relationship with the Word must be personal and transformative, shaping his own life before he can hope to shape the lives of others.

St. John Chrysostom emphasized the need for the priest to live a life worthy of his calling:

> "A priest is called to be as pure as if he were standing in heaven itself... for he offers the prayers of the people to God and offers to the people the Word of God" (*On the Priesthood, Book III*).

The priest's personal sanctification is essential for his ministry, as it enables him to be a faithful vessel through which God's Word can bear fruit in the lives of the faithful.

In St. Basil's Divine Liturgy, the priest prays for the grace to be a faithful servant of the Word:

> "You have called us to this holy service, O Lord, that we may offer You the praises of Your people and proclaim Your Word with truth and power."

This prayer reminds the priest that his teaching, preaching, and evangelizing are not his own work but the work of God, who uses the priest as His instrument.

## Conclusion

The priest's role as a teacher, preacher, and evangelizer is central to his ministry. He is entrusted with the divine Word of God, called to proclaim it with power, teach it with clarity, and share it with zeal. His life, rooted in the Word, becomes a living witness to the transformative power of God's truth, leading others into deeper communion with Christ and His Church. As St. Gregory the Theologian prayed, the priest is called to preach and teach the Word so that the people may grow in knowledge of the truth and be sanctified by the saving message of the Gospel (John 17:17).

# Chapter 8

# The Priest as a Minister of Reconciliation

One of the most profound and sacred roles of the priest is his ministry as a reconciler, bringing the people of God back into the right relationship with Him through the sacrament of confession. In this sacrament, the priest becomes an instrument of God's mercy and grace, offering forgiveness to those who seek it with a repentant heart. The ministry of reconciliation is a central aspect of the priest's calling, as he participates in Christ's work of healing and restoring the souls of the faithful. This sacred duty reflects the love and care of God the Father, who, through Christ, reconciles the world to Himself (2 Corinthians 5:18-19).

In confession, the priest is entrusted with the authority to forgive sins—a power given not by human hands but by Christ Himself through the Holy Spirit. This sacred trust requires the priest to approach the ministry of reconciliation with deep humility and reverence.

## The Priest as a Channel of God's Mercy

The sacrament of confession is often described as a "second baptism," where the soul, burdened by sin, is cleansed and restored to its original purity. The priest, as a minister of this sacrament, serves as a channel through which God's mercy flows. He does not forgive sins by his power but by the authority given to him by Christ. As a father of confession, the priest stands with the authority given to him through Christ, listening to the penitent, guiding them in repentance, and offering absolution.

St. Basil's Divine Liturgy captures this truth in its prayers: "O God of mercy and compassion, You alone have the power to remit sins. We beseech You, through Your priests, to forgive the sins of those who confess their transgressions and seek Your mercy." This prayer acknowledges that it is God who forgives, but the priest is the one through whom this forgiveness is mediated, bringing the healing grace of Christ to the penitent soul.

The priest's role as a channel of mercy requires him to reflect the compassion and gentleness of Christ. As St. Ambrose of Milan taught,

> "The servant of the Lord must not quarrel; he must be kind towards all, apt to teach, patient when wronged, gentle, and able to correct opponents with meekness, so that they may come to repentance." (*On the Duties of the Clergy, Book II*).

In the confessional, the priest is called to embody these virtues, offering correction and guidance with kindness while leading the penitent toward genuine conversion of heart.

The priest's ministry is a continuation of Christ's mission to seek and save the lost (Luke 19:10). As a reflection of the Father's love, the priest's attitude should echo Christ's words in the parable of the prodigal son: "When he was still a great way off, his father saw him and had compassion and ran and fell on his neck and kissed him" (Luke 15:20). The priest's gentleness in confession embodies the Father's eagerness to restore those who return to Him.

## The Power and Authority to Forgive Sins

The power to forgive sins is one of the greatest gifts Christ bestowed upon His apostles and, by extension, upon the Church through the priesthood. After His resurrection, Jesus breathed on His disciples and said, "Receive the Holy Spirit. If you forgive the sins of any, they are forgiven them; if you retain the sins of any, they are retained" (John 20:22-23). The priest exercises this divine authority to forgive sins in the sacrament of confession, where he becomes an instrument of God's healing grace.

St. John Chrysostom marveled at the gravity of this authority:

> "The priests have received a power which God has given neither to angels nor to archangels. It was said to them: 'Whatsoever you shall bind on earth shall be bound in heaven, and whatsoever you shall loose on earth shall be loosed in heaven.' Earthly rulers indeed have the power of binding, but they can bind only the body. Priests, in contrast, can bind with a bond which pertains to the soul itself and transcends the heavens" (*On the Priesthood, Book III*).

St. Chrysostom's reflection underscores the immense spiritual authority vested in the priest during the sacrament of confession, as his words of absolution carry eternal consequences.

This power is not given for the sake of control but for the sake of healing and restoration. The priest is called to approach this responsibility with humility, recognizing that he is acting on behalf of Christ and that the forgiveness he offers is a manifestation of God's boundless mercy.

The priest's own experience of God's forgiveness allows him to approach the sacrament of confession with compassion and understanding, guiding the penitent toward true reconciliation with God. St. Gregory of Nazianzus emphasized,

> "We must be sanctified before sanctifying others; we must be forgiven before offering forgiveness." (*Oration 2, On the Priesthood*).

# Healing the Wounds of Sin

Sin wounds not only the soul but also the community of faith. When a member of the body of Christ sins, the entire body suffers (1 Corinthians 12:26). The sacrament of confession, therefore, is not only a personal encounter with God's mercy but also a means of restoring the penitent to communion with the Church. The priest, as a minister of reconciliation, is tasked with healing these wounds, offering spiritual guidance and penances that help the penitent grow in holiness and avoid future sin.

St. Basil's Divine Liturgy contains a prayer that reflects this healing role:

> "O Lord, the Physician of our souls and bodies, who know the hidden depths of our hearts, heal the wounds of our sins and restore us to Your grace, that we may walk in the light of Your truth."

The priest, acting as a spiritual physician, must apply the medicine of God's mercy to the wounds of sin, helping the penitent to experience true healing and conversion.

St. Gregory the Great, in his *Pastoral Rule*, spoke of the priest's responsibility to treat the wounds of sin with care:

> "The care of souls is like the treatment of wounds. The physician must be gentle in some cases and firm in others, knowing when to apply the salve of mercy and when to use the knife of correction."

The priest, as a spiritual physician, must discern the best way to lead each penitent toward healing, sometimes offering gentle encouragement and at other times issuing stern warnings. In all cases, the priest is called to act with love and concern for the well-being of the soul.

The priest's ministry mirrors Christ's healing touch, as seen when Jesus forgave sins and restored individuals to wholeness, such as the paralyzed man whom Jesus healed, saying, "Son, be of good cheer; your sins are forgiven you" (Matthew 9:2). Just as Jesus healed both body and soul, the priest's role is to help restore the spiritual health of those who come to confession.

## The Priest as a Guide to Repentance

Confession is not only about receiving forgiveness but also about fostering a spirit of repentance and conversion. The priest's role in the confessional is to guide the penitent toward a deeper relationship with God, helping them to recognize their sins, express genuine sorrow, and make a firm resolve to amend their lives. The priest is called to encourage the penitent to see confession not as a mere formality but as a transformative encounter with the mercy of God.

St. John Chrysostom emphasized the importance of repentance in the sacrament of confession:

> "Do not tell me that you have sinned many times and that you are full of wounds. Come to the physician. Show your wounds, and through confession, you will receive healing for your sins" (*Homilies on Matthew*).

St. Chrysostom's words highlight the healing power of confession, where repentance opens the door to God's grace and forgiveness. The priest's role is to foster this spirit of repentance in the penitent, helping them to approach the sacrament with a contrite heart and a desire for conversion.

In the Divine Liturgy of St. Basil, the priest prays:

> "Grant, O Lord, that those who come to You with repentant hearts may find mercy and forgiveness. Cleanse them from all their iniquities and restore them to Your grace, that they may walk in newness of life."

This prayer encapsulates the goal of the sacrament of confession: to restore the penitent to the grace of God and to lead them to a life of holiness. The priest's role is to guide the penitent on this journey of repentance, offering spiritual counsel and encouragement to help them grow in their relationship with God.

## The Joy of Reconciliation

While the sacrament of confession is often seen as a serious occasion, it is also a moment of great joy. When a sinner returns to God, the entire Church rejoices, and heaven itself celebrates the reconciliation of a lost soul. The priest, as a minister of reconciliation, shares in this joy, for he has been privileged to witness the transformative power of God's mercy in the lives of the faithful.

Jesus expressed this joy in the parable of the lost sheep: "There will be more joy in heaven over one sinner who repents than over ninety-nine just persons who need no repentance" (Luke 15:7). In offering absolution, the priest is not only acting as a judge but also as a joyful witness to the mercy of God, who desires that all sinners return to Him.

St. Gregory of Nazianzus wrote of the joy that accompanies the forgiveness of sins:

> "There is nothing more joyful than the restoration of a soul to God. The angels in heaven rejoice, and the Church on earth sings praises, for a soul that was lost has been found, a sinner has been reconciled to God." (*Oration 39, On the Feast of Theophany*).

In the Divine Liturgy of St. Cyril of Alexandria, this joy is reflected in the priest's prayers of thanksgiving:

> "We thank You, O Lord, for Your boundless mercy, for You do not desire the death of a sinner but that

they should turn from their ways and live. We praise You for the forgiveness of sins, for restoring us to Your grace, and for welcoming us into the joy of Your kingdom."

The priest's ministry of reconciliation is a cause for celebration, as it brings about the restoration of the soul to God's grace and opens the doors of heaven to those who seek mercy.

## Conclusion

The priest's role as a minister of reconciliation is one of the most sacred and life-giving aspects of his ministry. In the sacrament of confession, the priest acts as a channel of God's mercy, offering forgiveness to those who come with repentant hearts. He serves as a spiritual physician, healing the wounds of sin and guiding the faithful toward holiness and conversion. Through the authority given to him by Christ, the priest offers absolution, restoring the penitent to communion with God and the Church.

St. John Chrysostom's reflection on the priest's role in confession continues to inspire:

> "The priests have received a power which God has given neither to angels nor to archangels. It was said to them: 'Whatsoever you shall bind on earth shall be bound in heaven, and whatsoever you shall loose on earth shall be loosed in heaven.'"

In every act of absolution, the priest exercises this divine authority, bringing God's mercy and forgiveness to the faithful.

As ministers of reconciliation, priests are called to be instruments of God's healing grace, helping the faithful to experience the joy of being restored to God's love. Through the sacrament of confession, the priest plays a vital role in the spiritual life of the Church, leading the people of God into the fullness of life in Christ.

# Chapter 9

# The Priest's Liturgical Life

The priest stands at the heart of the Church's worship, leading the people of God into the sacred mysteries and offering their prayers and sacrifices to the Lord. Through the celebration of the Divine Liturgy, the priest enters into the presence of God, facilitating the communion of heaven and earth. The liturgical life of the priest is central to his calling, as it is through the liturgy that the priest participates in the sanctification of the faithful and the ongoing work of salvation. In this sacred duty, the priest reflects the love and care of God the Father, revealed through Christ, the eternal High Priest.

St. John Chrysostom emphasizes the profound nature of this role:

> "When you behold the Lord sacrificed and laid upon the altar, and the priest standing and praying, and all the worshipers empurpled with that precious blood, do you then imagine that you are still among men, and standing upon the earth? Are you not, on the contrary, immediately transported to heaven?" (*On the Priesthood, Book III*).

This vivid description reminds us that the priest, in his liturgical role, transcends the ordinary and leads the people into the very presence of God, where His love and care are most powerfully revealed.

## The Priest as Mediator Between God and His People

The priest's role in the liturgy is one of mediation through Christ. Just as Christ mediates between God and humanity (1 Timothy 2:5), the priest stands as a bridge, offering the prayers of the people to God and bringing God's grace to the people through the sacraments. His presence at the altar reflects the ministry of Christ, who, as the High Priest, offered Himself for the salvation of the world (Hebrews 9:11-14).

In the Divine Liturgy of St. Cyril of Alexandria, the priest prays:

> "O Master, Lord, the Father of mercies and God of all comfort, we give thanks to You, who have made us worthy to stand in this holy place, to serve as priests of Your altar, and to be the ministers of Your holy mysteries."

This prayer reflects the priest's profound gratitude for the gift of his ministry, recognizing that his role as a mediator in the liturgy is a grace bestowed by God, not something earned by personal merit. The priest stands at the altar as a servant of God, offering the prayers and sacrifices of the people in union with the one sacrifice of Christ.

The priest, as a mediator, must first draw near to God himself. His leadership in the liturgy is not merely a ritual duty but a spiritual responsibility, requiring him to cultivate holiness in his own life so that he can effectively bring others into God's presence.

## The Eucharist: The Heart of the Liturgical Life

At the center of the priest's liturgical life is the celebration of the Eucharist; it is the moment when the priest, acting in the person of Christ, offers the sacrifice of the Mass, bringing Christ's saving work on the cross into the present and making it available to the faithful. The priest's role in this sacred act is both humbling and awe-inspiring as he participates in the divine mystery of salvation.

St. Cyril of Alexandria's Divine Liturgy beautifully expresses this mystery:

> "For You, O Lord, are He who offers and He who is offered, He who receives and He who is distributed. You, O Christ our God, are the sacrifice that we present and the One whom we receive in communion."

This passage highlights the profound reality that Christ is both the priest and the sacrifice in the Eucharist. In offering the Eucharist, the priest participates in Christ's eternal priesthood (Hebrews 7:24-25).

St. John Chrysostom also reflects on the majesty of the Eucharist:

> "What the priest does here, Christ Himself does there: He offers the sacrifice. Yes, the same one that was offered once and for all, not many times, but the same. Therefore, do not be deceived that the Eucharist is just a symbol — it is a real participation in the sacrifice of Christ" (*Homilies on Hebrews*).

St. Chrysostom's teaching emphasizes that the Eucharist is not merely a representation but a true participation in the sacrifice of Christ. In celebrating the Eucharist, the priest leads the people into the mystery of Christ's death and resurrection, making present the saving grace of God, revealed in Christ's ultimate act of love on the cross.

## Leading the People in Worship

The priest's liturgical leadership is not limited to the Eucharist. He is also responsible for leading the people in the daily prayer of the Church, administering the sacraments, and presiding over the various liturgical rites that mark the Christian life. From baptisms and weddings to funerals and anointings, the priest's role is to lead the people in offering their lives to God, sanctifying the moments of life through the grace of the sacraments (Ephesians 5:26-27).

St. Basil's Divine Liturgy reflects the priest's responsibility to lead the people in prayer and worship:

> "We pray You, O Lord our God, remember all Your people and all Your Church. Pour out the riches of Your mercy and compassion on them. Preserve them in peace and guard them under the shadow of Your wings."

This prayer highlights the priest's role as an intercessor for the people, offering their prayers to God and seeking His protection and guidance for the Church.

The priest's leadership in worship is about creating an environment where the people can encounter God's presence, love, and care. This requires the priest to lead with reverence and devotion, ensuring that the liturgy is celebrated with the dignity and beauty that reflect the glory of God.

St. John Chrysostom warned priests not to treat the liturgy as a mere obligation:

> "Do not approach the altar lightly, as if you are performing a routine duty. Instead, approach with fear and trembling, recognizing the holiness of what you are about to do" (*On the Priesthood, Book III*).

The priest is always called to remember that he is standing before the throne of God, leading the people in worship that transcends the earthly and reflects the heavenly.

## Liturgical Life as a Model of Holiness

The priest's liturgical life is not just about performing religious rituals; it is about leading the people into the holiness of God. Through the liturgy, the priest sanctifies the people, bringing them into the presence of God and helping them grow in their relationship with Him. The priest, in his role as a liturgical leader, must embody the holiness he seeks to impart to others, serving as a model of prayer, reverence, and devotion.

The priest cannot lead others into the presence of God if he is not striving for his own holiness. His own prayer life, devotion, and purity of heart are essential for the effectiveness of his liturgical leadership.

In the Liturgy of St. Basil, the priest prays:

> "Purify our hearts, O Lord, that we may offer You this sacrifice without blemish, that it may be acceptable in Your sight, and that we may be counted worthy of Your heavenly kingdom."

This prayer reminds the priest that his own purity and holiness are integral to his ability to lead the people in worship. The priest's liturgical life must be rooted in his personal holiness, as he serves not only as a leader of the liturgy but as an example of how to live a life of worship.

# Liturgical Life as a Participation in Heavenly Liturgy

The liturgy celebrated by the priest is not an isolated event; it is a participation in the eternal worship of heaven. When the priest celebrates the liturgy, he joins the angels and saints in offering praise and glory to God. This reality transforms the priest's liturgical role into something far greater than a mere earthly duty—it is an invitation to participate in the heavenly liturgy, where God the Father through Christ is forever worshiped by the hosts of heaven (Revelation 4:8-11).

St. Basil's Divine Liturgy reflects this profound truth:

> "With these blessed powers, O Master, who loves mankind, we also cry aloud and say: Holy are You and all-holy, You and Your only begotten Son and Your Holy Spirit! Holy are You and all-holy, and magnificent is Your glory, who has so loved Your world as to give Your only begotten Son, that whoever believes in Him should not perish but have eternal life."

This prayer connects the earthly liturgy with the heavenly worship, reminding the priest that he is not only offering worship on behalf of the people but also joining with the angels in glorifying God.

St. John Chrysostom emphasized the unity between the earthly and heavenly liturgies:

> "When you are offering the sacrifice, think that you are not doing so on earth, but that you are already in heaven. When you see the priest offering the holy sacrifice, think that an angel stands by him and that the whole sanctuary and space around the altar is filled with heavenly powers" (*On the Priesthood, Book III*).

The priest, in his liturgical role, transcends time and space, entering into the eternal worship of God that takes place in heaven. This awareness transforms the priest's understanding of the liturgy, reminding him of the sacred and divine nature of his ministry.

## Conclusion

The priest's liturgical life is at the heart of his ministry. As an intercessor between God and His people, the priest leads the faithful into the presence of God, offering their prayers and sacrifices in union with Christ. The Eucharist is the central act of the priest's liturgical ministry, but his role extends beyond the

Eucharist to all the sacraments and liturgical rites of the Church. In leading worship, the priest not only prays for the sanctification of the people but also participates in the eternal liturgy of heaven, joining the angels and saints in offering praise and glory to God.

St. John Chrysostom's words continue to inspire priests today:

> "Do not approach the altar lightly, as if you are performing a routine duty. Instead, approach with fear and trembling, recognizing the holiness of what you are about to do."

The priest's liturgical life is not simply a function of his ministry; it is a sacred duty that calls him to holiness, reverence, and devotion. In leading the people in worship, the priest fulfills his role as a servant of God, an instrument of grace, and a participant in the heavenly worship that will continue eternally.

# Chapter 10

# The Priest as the Celebrant of the Eucharist

At the heart of the priestly ministry lies the celebration of the Eucharist; it is not merely a ritual or a commemoration, but the living sacrifice of Christ made present to His Church. For the priest, the Eucharist is the highest expression of his ministry, for it is in the Eucharist that he acts in the person of Christ, offering the Body and Blood of Christ for the salvation of the world. In this act, the priest becomes a vital instrument of God's grace, bringing the faithful into communion with Christ through the most profound of the Church's sacraments. This mirrors the love and care of God the Father, who gave His Son as a sacrifice for the salvation of humanity (John 3:16).

St. Chrysostom's words remind us that the Eucharist is the same sacrifice that Christ offered on the cross, and through the priest's ministry, this sacrifice is made present for the people of God.

## The Priest as a Minister of the Eucharistic Sacrifice

The priest's role in the celebration of the Eucharist is unique. He is not merely a presider over a ceremony but stands at the altar as a representative of Christ, offering the same sacrifice that Christ offered for the redemption of the world. This is the central mystery of the priesthood: that the priest, by the power of the Holy Spirit, is able to make present the Body and Blood of Christ under the forms of bread and wine. In this sacred act, the priest participates in Christ's eternal priesthood, offering the sacrifice of the Mass for the salvation of the world (Hebrews 9:11-14).

St. Cyril of Alexandria's Divine Liturgy expresses the profundity of this act:

> "For You, O Lord, are He who offers and He who is offered, He who receives and He who is distributed. You, O Christ our God, are the sacrifice that we present and the One whom we receive in communion."

This liturgical text highlights the mystery of the Eucharist, where Christ is both the priest and the sacrifice, the one who offers the sacrifice and the one who is offered in sacrifice. By celebrating the Eucharist, the priest enters into this mystery, standing in the place of Christ to offer His saving sacrifice for the people.

In this sense, the priest mirrors Christ's self-giving love and the Father's compassionate care for His people, acting as an intermediary who offers the people's sacrifices and petitions to God. As the Letter to the Hebrews reminds us, "Every high priest is appointed to offer both gifts and sacrifices. Therefore, it is necessary that this One also have something to offer" (Hebrews 8:3). The priest's role is to stand before God on behalf of the people, continuing the work of Christ, the ultimate High Priest.

## The Eucharist as the Center of the Priest's Life

For the priest, the Eucharist is not only the central act of his ministry but also the source of his spiritual life. The priest is called to draw his strength, wisdom, and love from the Eucharist, which nourishes his soul and sustains him in his ministry. Every time the priest celebrates the Eucharist, he is reminded of Christ's sacrifice and is invited to unite his life and ministry to the self-giving love of Christ, reflecting the Father's love for the world.

In the Divine Liturgy of St. Basil, the priest prays:

"Grant us, O Lord, to stand before Your holy altar and to offer this bloodless sacrifice for our sins and the sins of all Your people. Fill us with Your Holy Spirit, that we may offer this sacrifice with a pure heart and be united to You in love and holiness."

This prayer reflects the intimate connection between the priest's spiritual life and the celebration of the Eucharist. The Eucharist not only sanctifies the people but also sanctifies the priest, drawing him deeper into communion with God and transforming him through the power of Christ's sacrifice by the Holy Spirit.

The priest's life must be rooted in the Eucharist, for it is from the Eucharist that he receives the grace and strength to carry out his ministry. The priest cannot lead others into communion with Christ if the Eucharist is not constantly nourishing him himself. As Jesus declared, "I am the bread of life. He who comes to Me shall never hunger, and he who believes in Me shall never thirst" (John 6:35). The priest, too, must continually feed on this bread to sustain his soul and ministry.

# The Priest as a Servant of the Eucharistic Community

The Eucharist is not only a personal encounter with Christ; it is also the sacrament of communion, uniting the faithful with one another as the Body of Christ. In celebrating the Eucharist, the priest serves as a steward of this unity, gathering the people of God around the altar and offering the sacrifice of Christ on their behalf. The priest's role in the Eucharist is not just to administer the sacrament but to foster a sense of communion within the Church, helping the faithful to recognize that they are united as one body through their participation in the Body and Blood of Christ.

St. Paul teaches this reality in his First Letter to the Corinthians: "Because there is one bread, we who are many are one body, for we all partake of the one bread" (1 Corinthians 10:17). The Eucharist is the source of the Church's unity, and as the one who offers the Eucharist, the priest is responsible for building and maintaining this unity within the community. His leadership at the altar is a visible sign of the Church's unity in Christ, and his care for the Eucharistic community reflects the self-giving love of Christ, the Good Shepherd (John 10:11).

St. Basil's Divine Liturgy emphasizes the communal aspect of the Eucharist:

> "We thank You, O Lord, for having counted us worthy to stand in Your holy presence and to offer to You this sacrifice of praise. Unite us all, who partake of this one bread and one cup, that we may be one body in Christ and serve You with love and peace."

This prayer highlights the Eucharist as the sacrament of unity, bringing together the faithful in love and peace.

The priest's role is to serve this Eucharistic community, helping the faithful to grow in their communion with one another and with God. His ministry, centered on the Eucharist, thus reflects the Father's desire for all His children to be united in love and peace (John 17:21).

## Eucharist as a Sacrifice of Thanksgiving

The word "Eucharist" itself means "thanksgiving," and at its core, the celebration of the Eucharist is an offering of thanks to God for His abundant blessings, especially the gift of salvation through Jesus Christ. The priest, as the celebrant of the Eucharist, leads the people in this act of thanksgiving, offering the Church's praise and gratitude to God. This offering of thanks is not simply a verbal expression but is embodied in the sacrificial offering of Christ's Body and Blood, which is the ultimate act of thanksgiving to the Father.

St. John Chrysostom reflected on the Eucharist as a sacrifice of thanksgiving:

> "For what else is the Eucharist but a thanksgiving to God? When we offer the Eucharist, we are giving thanks for everything—for creation, for redemption, for the hope of eternal life. This is the sacrifice of praise that we offer to God, who has given us all things" (*Homilies on Matthew*).

In celebrating the Eucharist, the priest leads the people in this act of thanksgiving, offering praise to God for the gift of Christ's sacrifice and the hope of eternal life.

In the Divine Liturgy of St. Basil, this spirit of thanksgiving is evident:

> "We give thanks to You, O Lord, for Your many and great blessings, which we have received at Your hands. Above all, we give thanks for the precious Body and Blood of Christ, which You have given us for the life of the world."

The priest's celebration of the Eucharist is a continuous act of thanksgiving, acknowledging God's generosity and mercy and offering the Church's praise and gratitude for the gift of salvation.

# The Priest as a Participant in the Heavenly Liturgy

When the priest celebrates the Eucharist, he is not simply performing an earthly rite; he is participating in the eternal liturgy of heaven, where Christ is forever offering Himself to the Father on behalf of humanity. The Eucharist is a foretaste of the heavenly banquet. In celebrating this sacred mystery, the priest joins the angels and saints in offering worship and praise to God. This heavenly dimension of the Eucharist transforms the priest's understanding of his role, reminding him that he is not only ministering to the people of God on earth but also participating in the worship of heaven.

St. Basil's Divine Liturgy expresses this heavenly reality:

> "With these blessed powers, O Master, who loves mankind, we also cry aloud and say: Holy are You and all-holy, You and Your only begotten Son and Your Holy Spirit! Holy are You and all-holy, and magnificent is Your glory, who has so loved Your world as to give Your only begotten Son, that whoever believes in Him should not perish but have eternal life."

In this prayer, the priest acknowledges that the Eucharist is not merely an earthly event but a participation in the eternal worship of God, where the Church on earth is united with the Church in heaven.

St. John Chrysostom also emphasized this heavenly aspect of the Eucharist:

> "When you see the priest standing before the altar, think not that he is performing this work alone. Around him are all the heavenly powers, and with him, they sing the hymn of praise to God. The Eucharist is the union of heaven and earth, where the angels and saints join us in worship" (*On the Priesthood, Book III*).

The priest's role in the Eucharist is thus elevated to a cosmic scale, where he joins the entire heavenly host in offering praise and thanksgiving to God.

# Conclusion

The Eucharist is the source and summit of the priest's life and ministry. In celebrating the Eucharist, the priest not only offers the sacrifice of Christ for the salvation of the world but also draws his own life and strength from the same sacrifice. The Eucharist is the center of the priest's spiritual life, nourishing him in holiness and sustaining him in his ministry. It is through the Eucharist that the priest fulfills his role as a mediator between God and His people, uniting the Church in communion with Christ and one another.

St. John Chrysostom's reflection on the Eucharist continues to inspire priests today:

> "What the priest does here, Christ Himself does there: He offers the sacrifice. Yes, the same one that was offered once and for all, not many times, but the same."

In every celebration of the Eucharist, the priest enters into the mystery of Christ's sacrifice, participating in the eternal liturgy of heaven and offering the gift of salvation to the people of God. This is the heart of the priest's ministry, and it is through the Eucharist that the priest finds his deepest identity and purpose.

# Chapter 11

# The Priest and the Church: Unity, Authority, and Service

The priest serves not only as a spiritual guide for individual believers but also as a key figure within the larger body of Christ—the Church. His ministry is intimately connected to the life of the Church, and his authority and responsibilities are rooted in the unity and mission of the Church. This chapter explores the priest's role within the Church, his relationship with ecclesiastical authority, and his responsibility to foster unity within the Christian community.

## The Priest as a Representative of the Church

The priest is not an isolated figure; he functions as a representative of the Church, acting in communion with the bishop and the wider Church body. His ministry is an extension of the Church's mission to proclaim the Gospel, celebrate the sacraments, and guide the faithful toward holiness. In every aspect of his ministry, the priest represents the Church, and through his actions, words, and pastoral care, he reveals the Church's love and care for God's people.

St. John Chrysostom highlighted the priest's role as a representative of the Church:

> "The priest does not act of his own accord but as an ambassador of Christ and His Church. He carries the authority of the Church, and in every word and deed, he must reflect the mission of the Church to bring souls to salvation." (*On the Priesthood, Book V*).

This emphasizes that the priest's authority comes not from himself but from the Church, and his ministry is a participation in the Church's work of salvation.

The priest's ordination consecrates him to act in the person of Christ and in the person of the Church. His ministry, therefore, is not about personal ambition or individual authority but about serving Christ and the Church faithfully. As Christ represents the Father's love for humanity, the priest represents Christ and the Church's mission to lead souls to eternal life.

St. Paul's words to the Ephesians express the unity of the Church's mission: "There is one body and one Spirit, just as you were called in one hope of your calling; one Lord, one faith, one baptism; one God and Father of all, who is above all, and through all, and in you all" (Ephesians 4:4-6). The priest's work is always in harmony with this unified mission, strengthening the bonds of faith, love, and service within the Church.

## The Priest's Relationship with the Bishop

One of the most important aspects of the priest's ministry is his relationship with the bishop. The bishop, as a successor to the apostles, holds the fullness of apostolic authority within the diocese, and the priest shares in this ministry by virtue of his ordination. The priest's role is to assist the bishop in shepherding the diocese, working in unity with him to care for the people of God.

St. Ignatius of Antioch emphasized the importance of the priest's relationship with the bishop:

> "Let all reverence the bishop as Jesus Christ, and the deacons as the apostolic ministry, and let the presbyters be esteemed as the council of God and the bond of unity with the bishop" (*Letter to the Smyrnaeans*).

The priest's relationship with the bishop is one of obedience, respect, and collaboration, as it is rooted in the apostolic mission of the Church.

Obedience to the bishop is not about submission to human authority but about honoring the divinely instituted order of the Church. The bishop, as a successor of the apostles, carries the responsibility of preserving the faith and ensuring the mission of the Church is carried out faithfully in every parish. The priest's role is to work under this apostolic authority, contributing to the Church's unity and mission.

Through this relationship, the priest remains connected to the wider Church. His obedience is a reflection of Christ's obedience to the Father (John 5:19), and this submission serves the greater good of the community. The collaboration between the bishop and priest mirrors the early Church's apostolic structure, where authority and service were inseparable, ensuring the Church remained united in faith and mission.

## Fostering Unity within the Parish

One of the priest's primary responsibilities is to foster unity within the parish community. The Church is called to be a sign of unity in a divided world, and the priest plays a central role in promoting this unity through his leadership, teaching, and pastoral care. The priest is called to work to ensure that the parish reflects the oneness of the body of Christ, where all members are united in faith, love, and service.

St. Gregory the Great emphasized the priest's role in promoting unity:

> "The priest is called to be a builder of peace and unity, for without unity, the Church cannot stand. It is his calling to reconcile, to heal divisions, and to lead the people to a deeper understanding of their oneness in Christ" (*Pastoral Rule*).

The priest is called to be vigilant in fostering a spirit of love and harmony among parishioners, ensuring that conflicts are addressed with wisdom and compassion.

The Eucharist is the primary source of this unity. When the priest celebrates the Eucharist, he not only offers the sacrifice of Christ but also draws the community together in a profound act of communion. St. Paul teaches, "For we, though many, are one bread and one body; for we all partake of that one bread" (1 Corinthians 10:17). In the Eucharist, the faithful are united with Christ and with one another, and the priest serves as the visible sign of this unity.

The priest's role in fostering Eucharistic devotion and reverence helps to strengthen the bonds of unity within the parish. His ministry ensures that the Eucharist remains the source and summit of parish life, where the faithful encounter Christ and are drawn together as one body. The priest is also called to promote a spirit of service, encouraging parishioners to live out their faith in love and solidarity with one another.

## The Priest's Authority in Teaching and Stewardship

The priest's authority within the Church extends beyond pastoral care to include teaching and stewardship. As a teacher of the faith, the priest is entrusted with the responsibility of ensuring that the truths of the Gospel are faithfully proclaimed and that the teachings of the Church are upheld. This authority is exercised not for personal gain but for the edification of the people of God.

St. John Chrysostom spoke of the priest's duty to teach the faith with clarity and authority:

> "The priest is a steward of the mysteries of God, and it is his sacred duty to teach the people the truths of the Gospel. His words must be rooted in Scripture and Tradition, and he must ensure that the people are nourished by sound doctrine" (*Homilies on Acts*).

St. Chrysostom's words highlight the importance of faithful teaching in the priest's ministry, ensuring that the truths of the faith are passed on with diligence and care.

The priest's authority in stewardship also plays a key role in the life of the parish. As the spiritual leader of the community, the priest is responsible for overseeing the administration of the parish, managing its resources, and ensuring that its ministries and programs align with the Church's mission. This role extends the priest's spiritual leadership, where the wisdom and integrity of his stewardship contribute to the flourishing of the parish.

The priest's stewardship is always rooted in service, mirroring Christ's words: "Whoever desires to become great among you, let him be your servant" (Matthew 20:26). By leading with humility and love, the priest creates an environment where the faithful can grow in holiness, and the Church's mission can be fulfilled.

## Working Together with the Faithful

While the priest holds a unique position of authority within the Church, his ministry is also one of working together with the faithful. St. Basil emphasized the need for unity between the ordained ministers and the members of Christ's body:

> "The Church is the body of Christ, and each member has a vital role to play. The priest's task is to guide and empower the faithful to fulfill their calling, for without their participation, the Church cannot fully live out its mission." (*Homilies on the Psalms*).

The priest's role is to equip the faithful, helping them recognize and develop their gifts and callings within the Church.

Working together also involves listening to the needs and concerns of the faithful, seeking their counsel, and building relationships of trust and respect. The priest is called to labor alongside the faithful to create a parish community where all are engaged in the Church's mission of evangelization, service, and worship. The priest's ability to work harmoniously with the faithful enhances the parish's vitality and helps the Church to fulfill its mission in the world.

## The Priest and the Universal Church

While the priest's ministry is often focused on the local parish or diocese, he is also part of the universal Church. His ministry connects him to the wider body of Christ, which spans across nations, cultures, and generations. This connection to the universal Church reminds the priest that his ministry is part of a greater mission that extends beyond his immediate context.

St. Cyril of Alexandria reflected on the priest's connection to the universal Church:

> "The priest's ministry is not limited to the local community, for he serves the one Church of Christ, which encompasses all peoples and nations. His role is to be a faithful servant of the Church's mission, ensuring that his ministry reflects the universality of the Gospel" (*Homilies on the Gospel of John*).

The priest's relationship with the universal Church helps to preserve the unity of the faith and ensures that his ministry is grounded in the fullness of the wider body of Christ.

## Conclusion

The priest's ministry is deeply rooted in the life of the Church. As a representative of the Church, the priest serves in communion with the bishop and the wider body of Christ, fostering unity within the parish and exercising his authority with humility and grace. His role as a spiritual leader involves both pastoral care and stewardship, ensuring that the truths of the faith are faithfully proclaimed and that the parish is guided in its pursuit of holiness. By working with the faithful and remaining connected to the universal Church, the priest fulfills his mission to serve the people of God and to build up the body of Christ in love and unity.

# Chapter 12

# The Priest's Role in His Family

The life of a priest is often seen as a ministry primarily directed towards the Church, but it is essential to acknowledge the vital role a priest plays within his own family. In the Orthodox Church and certain rites of the Catholic Church, priests are not only spiritual fathers to their congregations but also husbands, fathers, and even grandfathers. This unique calling requires the priest to balance his responsibilities within the Church and his home, living out his calling in a way that brings grace, love, and spiritual strength to both spheres. This chapter examines the priest's role within his family, highlighting how his ministry at home complements and enhances his ministry in the Church.

## The Priest as a Husband: A Covenant of Love and Unity

The priest's role as a husband begins with his commitment to love and support his wife. The marital bond is not only a social contract but a sacramental union, blessed by God and a reflection of Christ's relationship with the Church. St. Paul writes, "Husbands, love your wives, just as Christ also loved the church and gave Himself for her" (Ephesians 5:25). His profound call to sacrificial love is at the heart of the priest's marriage. His relationship with his wife should exemplify mutual respect, understanding, and self-giving love.

As a spiritual leader, the priest models Christ-like love within his marriage. This love is not merely expressed in words but in daily acts of care, patience, and selflessness. His dedication to his wife sets an example for his parishioners, showing them how to live out their own marriage covenant. By prioritizing his relationship with his wife, the priest demonstrates that love, commitment, and unity are central to every Christian household. In the marriage, the priest and his wife are partners, supporting each other in their spiritual journey and in the responsibilities of ministry, which can often be demanding and challenging.

## The Priest as a Father: Nurturing Faith at Home

The priest's fatherhood is both spiritual and biological, and his role as a father extends beyond his congregation to his children. As a father, he is called to be a guide, protector, and teacher, nurturing his children's faith and leading them by example. The Book of Proverbs advises, "Train up a child in the way he should go, And when he is old he will not depart from it" (Proverbs 22:6). The priest, as a father, takes on this responsibility, instilling in his children a love for God, a commitment to prayer, and a desire to live according to the teachings of the Gospel.

In his home, the priest creates an environment where faith is not just practiced on Sundays but integrated into daily life. Family prayers, scripture readings, and discussions about God become a regular part of the household, providing a strong spiritual foundation for the children. The priest's role as a father is to foster an atmosphere of love, warmth, and encouragement, where each family member feels valued and supported in their spiritual journey. His ability to balance the demands of ministry with his responsibilities at home teaches his children about the importance of service, sacrifice, and devotion.

## The Family as a Church: A Reflection of the Larger Community

The priest's home is often referred to as a "domestic church," a small reflection of the larger parish community. Just as the priest seeks to build unity, love, and holiness within his congregation, he is also called to cultivate these same virtues within his family. St. John Chrysostom, in his teachings on family life, emphasized that the home should be a place of worship, teaching, and mutual care. He wrote,

> "The home must be a little church, where the family gathers together, prays together and grows together in faith."

The priest's leadership in the family involves guiding them in spiritual practices, such as regular participation in the Church's liturgical life, observing feasts, and engaging in acts of charity. His family becomes an extension of his ministry, where his wife and children actively participate in the life of the Church, offering their support and service to the community. This integration of family and ministry enables the priest to lead by example, demonstrating that the values of faith, love, and service are instilled at home.

## Intercessory Prayer: Entrusting the Family to God's Care

A critical aspect of the priest's role in his family is his ministry of intercessory prayer, particularly during the offering of the Eucharist. As he stands before the altar, the priest brings not only the needs of his congregation but also the intentions and well-being of his own family to God. This act of prayer is a profound expression of the priest's love and concern for his family, as he entrusts each member to the care of the Shepherd of all souls.

During the Divine Liturgy, the priest has a special opportunity to lift up his wife, children, and even grandchildren in prayer, asking God to protect, bless, and guide them. This practice of intercessory prayer enables the priest to fulfill his role as both a spiritual and biological father, covering his family with grace and seeking God's presence in their lives. The prayers offered at the altar are an assurance that, despite the challenges and responsibilities of ministry, the priest's family remains enveloped in God's love and protection.

St. Basil's Divine Liturgy reflects this spirit of intercession:

> "Remember, O Lord, all those whom we have in mind and all our families. Protect, guide, and shelter them under Your loving care."

The priest's prayer at the altar becomes a moment of deep spiritual connection, uniting his love for God with his love for his family and ensuring that they are always included in the grace that flows from the Eucharistic celebration.

## Challenges and Blessings: Balancing Ministry and Family Life

One of the significant challenges for a priest is striking a balance between their duties to the Church and their responsibilities at home. The demands of pastoral ministry can often be overwhelming, with long hours, emotional burdens, and unexpected situations that require his immediate attention. However, the priest must recognize that his family is also his ministry. Just as he tends to the spiritual needs of his parish, he must also be attentive to the needs of his wife and children, ensuring that they feel loved, supported, and valued.

St. Paul also encourages, "If anyone does not provide for his own, and especially for those of his household, he has denied the faith and is worse than an unbeliever" (1 Timothy 5:8). This verse serves as a solemn reminder that the priest's duty to care for his family is not secondary to his ministry but a fundamental aspect of his faith and calling. In prioritizing the well-being of his household, he demonstrates the same love, care, and responsibility that he is called to extend to his parishioners.

St. Gregory of Nazianzus, in his reflections on the priesthood, acknowledged the challenges of balancing ministry and family life but emphasized that both are integral to the priest's calling. He wrote,

> "The priest's life is a life of service, both to his flock and to his own household. He must be vigilant, ensuring that he does not neglect one for the other, but rather sees both as sacred duties entrusted to him by God."

By maintaining this balance, the priest not only fulfills his responsibilities but also teaches his parishioners the importance of family life within the Christian faith.

The blessings of a priest's family life are profound. His wife, as a partner in ministry, often shares in the pastoral work, offering counsel, hospitality, and support to the parishioners. His children, raised in a home where faith is lived out daily, become witnesses to the love and grace of God. Through their involvement in the parish, the priest's family becomes a living example of the Christian virtues of love, service, and unity, inspiring others to follow the same path.

## The Priest's Family as a Witness to the Community

The priest's family is not just a private matter; it serves as a public witness to the community. Parishioners look to the priest's family as an example of Christian living, drawing inspiration from the way they interact, support each other, and live out their faith. This visibility can sometimes bring pressure, but it also provides an opportunity for the priest and his family to model the values of love, respect, and mutual care that are at the heart of the Gospel.

St. Paul's words to Timothy can be applied to the priest's family life: "He must manage his own family well and see that his children obey him, and he must do so in a manner worthy of full respect" (1 Timothy 3:4, NIV). The priest's ability to lead his family with love and wisdom reflects his ability to lead his parish. His home becomes a place of welcome, where parishioners can see the beauty of family life rooted in faith and where the love of Christ is made tangible through everyday interactions.

## Conclusion

The priest's role in his family is a crucial aspect of his ministry, one that complements and strengthens his work within the Church. As a husband, father, and spiritual leader, the priest is called to live out his calling in a way that brings grace and unity to his home. His family life is a reflection of his ministry, a "domestic church" where faith is nurtured, love is shared, and the Gospel is lived out daily.

By embracing his role within the family, the priest sets an example for his parishioners, showing them that the values of Christian love, sacrifice, and service begin at home. His dedication to his family is not a distraction from his ministry but a vital part of it, one that enriches his pastoral work and provides a lasting witness to the community. In living out his stewardship within his family, the priest fulfills his calling as a shepherd, guiding both his flock and his loved ones toward the love and grace of God.

# Chapter 13

## Spiritual Warfare and Overcoming Trials

The life of a priest is not free from struggles, temptations, and spiritual warfare. In fact, the priest, as a servant of God and a leader of the people, often faces greater spiritual challenges than the average believer. His ministry puts him directly on the front lines of spiritual battle, where he faces both the weaknesses of the flesh and the attacks of the evil one, who aims to undermine his work and destroy his witness. The priest's holy ministry attracts the opposition of the devil, who seeks to discourage, tempt, and destroy the priest in his ministry. Like Christ, the priest is called to face temptations and endure trials, but with God's Spirit, he can overcome them and emerge victorious in his mission.

## The Priest's Struggles with Temptations

Like every Christian, the priest faces temptations that seek to draw him away from God and compromise his witness. However, because of his position as a shepherd of souls, the priest's temptations are often more intense. He may face temptations of pride, discouragement, or complacency, as well as the common temptations of the flesh and the world. The priest is called to be ever vigilant in guarding his heart and mind, relying on the Spirit of God to resist the temptations that threaten his soul.

St. John Chrysostom warned of the dangers of pride in the priest's life:

> "There is no sin that the devil loves more to sow in the hearts of priests than pride, for pride blinds the soul and separates it from God. The priest, who is called to be humble and selfless, must be especially on guard against this deadly vice, which can destroy

both his own soul and the souls entrusted to him." *(On the Priesthood, Book IV)*.

The priest is called to constantly examine his heart, humbling himself before God and seeking the grace to overcome pride, which can easily take root in the human heart.

St. Gregory the Great, in his *Pastoral Rule*, also spoke of the dangers of spiritual complacency:

> "The priest who grows complacent in his ministry and neglects his spiritual duties becomes easy prey for the devil. For it is in times of spiritual sloth that the enemy attacks with his greatest force, and the soul, unprepared for battle, falls into temptation."

St. Gregory's warning serves as a reminder that the priest is called to remain spiritually vigilant, always seeking to grow in his relationship with God and to fulfill his pastoral duties with diligence and care.

Jesus Himself was tempted in the wilderness after fasting for forty days and nights. The Gospel of Matthew records how Satan attempted to lure Him away from His mission by appealing to hunger, power, and pride. Yet, Christ overcame every temptation by relying on the Word of God, saying, "Man shall not live by bread alone, but by every word that proceeds from the mouth of God" (Matthew 4:4). The priest, too, must rely on Scripture and God's promises to overcome the temptations that assail him.

In the Divine Liturgy of St. Basil, the priest prays for the strength to overcome temptations:

> "O Lord, deliver us from the temptations that assail us, and preserve us by Your grace. Strengthen us with Your Holy Spirit, that we may stand firm

against the snares of the enemy and remain faithful to You in all things."[1]

This prayer reflects the priest's reliance on God's grace in his battle against temptation, recognizing that it is only by the power of the Holy Spirit that he can resist the devil and remain faithful to his vocation.

## Enduring Trials and Sufferings

In addition to temptations, the priest is called to endure various trials and sufferings as part of his ministry. These trials may come in the form of personal struggles, conflicts within the Church, or external opposition from the world.

In the Book of Sirach (Ecclesiasticus), "My son, if you come to serve the Lord, prepare yourself for trials" (Sirach 2:1, RSV). This verse is often quoted to encourage perseverance and readiness to face challenges when committing oneself to a life of serving God. It emphasizes the need for spiritual resilience and preparation when undertaking a dedicated path of faith.

The priest is often called to suffer for the sake of the Gospel, just as Christ suffered for the sake of humanity. These trials, though painful, are opportunities for the priest to grow in holiness and to share in the sufferings of Christ.

St. Paul's words to the Corinthians speak to the priest's calling to endure suffering: "We are hard pressed on every side, yet not crushed; we are perplexed, but not in despair; persecuted, but not forsaken; struck down, but not destroyed-- always carrying about in the body the dying of the Lord Jesus, that the life of Jesus also may be manifested in our body" (2 Corinthians 4:8-10). The priest, in his ministry, carries the cross

---

[1] The quoted passage is a paraphrase rather than a direct citation from the Divine Liturgy of St. Basil the Great. In the liturgy, there are prayers that ask for God's protection, strength, and deliverance from evil, but the specific wording provided does not directly match any exact line.

of Christ, enduring suffering and hardship so that the life of Christ may be revealed in him and his people.

St. Gregory of Nazianzus also spoke of the priest's call to suffer for the sake of the Gospel:

> "The priest is called to be ready to endure hardship and suffering, for his vocation is one of sacrifice. He must be willing to bear the weight of the cross, just as Christ bore it for us. For it is through suffering that the soul is purified, and through endurance that the priest's ministry is strengthened" (*Oration 2, On the Priesthood*).

St. Gregory's words remind us that the priest's suffering is not in vain; it is a means of sanctification and an opportunity for the priest to participate in Christ's redemptive work.

In the Divine Liturgy of St. Cyril of Alexandria, the priest prays for the strength to endure trials:

> "Grant, O Lord, that we may endure the trials and sufferings that come our way with patience and trust in Your providence. Strengthen us by Your grace, that we may bear our crosses with courage and faith, knowing that You are with us in our time of need."

This prayer reflects the priest's reliance on God's grace in the midst of suffering, trusting that God will provide the strength needed to endure every trial.

## The Priest's Battle Against Spiritual Forces

The priest, in his role as a spiritual shepherd, is engaged in a constant battle against the spiritual forces of darkness. The devil, knowing the influence and importance of the priest's ministry, seeks to attack and undermine him at every turn. This spiritual warfare requires the priest to be constantly vigilant, armed with the weapons of prayer, fasting, and the sacraments. The priest's battle is not only for his own soul but also for the souls of those entrusted to his care.

St. Paul reminded the Ephesians of the reality of spiritual warfare: "For we do not wrestle against flesh and blood, but against principalities, against powers, against the rulers of the darkness of this age, against spiritual hosts of wickedness in the heavenly places" (Ephesians 6:12). The priest, in his ministry, must recognize that his true battle is not against human opposition but against the spiritual powers of darkness that seek to destroy the Church.

St. John Chrysostom spoke of the priest's battle against the devil:

> "The priest stands as a guardian at the gates of the Church, protecting the flock from the attacks of the enemy. He must be ever watchful, for the devil is constantly seeking to devour the souls of the faithful. The priest's weapons are not of this world but are the weapons of prayer, fasting, and the Word of God, by which he overcomes the powers of darkness." (*On the Priesthood, Book V*).

St. Chrysostom's words remind us that the priest's primary defense against the devil is his spiritual life, which must be grounded in prayer and the sacraments.

In the Divine Liturgy of St. Gregory the Theologian, the priest prays for protection in spiritual warfare:

> "Preserve us, O Lord, from the attacks of the enemy, and protect us from the powers of darkness. Strengthen us in this spiritual battle, that we may stand firm against the devil's schemes and remain faithful to Your holy calling."

This prayer reflects the priest's reliance on God's protection in the midst of spiritual warfare, recognizing that victory comes through God's grace and power.

## Overcoming Through God's Grace

Despite the many temptations, trials, and spiritual battles that the priest faces, he is not without hope. God's Spirit is always available to strengthen and sustain the priest in his struggles. Through prayer, the sacraments, and the support of the Church, the priest can overcome every challenge and remain faithful to his ministry. The priest's confidence is not in his own strength but in the power of God, who is always with him, guiding and protecting him in his ministry.

St. Paul's words to the Corinthians provide comfort and encouragement for the priest: "'My grace is sufficient for you, for My strength is made perfect in weakness.' Therefore most gladly I will rather boast in my infirmities, that the power of Christ may rest upon me" (2 Corinthians 12:9). The priest, though weak in himself, is made strong through the grace of God, who works through his weaknesses to accomplish His will.

St. Basil's Divine Liturgy reflects the priest's reliance on God's grace:

> "We give thanks to You, O Lord, for Your grace and mercy, which sustain us in all our trials. Grant that we may always trust in Your power and remain faithful to Your calling, knowing that Your grace is sufficient for every need."

This prayer reflects the priest's confidence in God's grace, which is always sufficient to sustain him in his ministry, no matter the struggles or challenges he may face. The priest's ultimate victory in spiritual warfare and his perseverance through trials are made possible by the power of God's Spirit, which enables him to fulfill his sacred ministry with faith and strength.

## The Role of Prayer and the Sacraments in Spiritual Warfare

The priest's primary means of overcoming temptations and spiritual attacks are found in the weapons of prayer and the sacraments. Through these divine gifts, the priest is strengthened by the grace of God, which fortifies him in his battle against the forces of darkness. Prayer is the priest's constant companion, helping him remain united with God and attentive to His will. The sacraments, especially the Eucharist and confession, provide the spiritual nourishment and healing needed to sustain the priest in his struggles.

St. Gregory the Great emphasized the importance of prayer in the priest's life:

> "The priest is called to be a man of constant prayer, for it is through prayer that he draws down the grace of God to protect himself and his people. Without prayer, the priest becomes vulnerable to the attacks of the devil and cannot fulfill his ministry with power" (*Pastoral Rule*).

Prayer is not optional for the priest; it is essential to his spiritual survival and effectiveness in ministry.

The Divine Liturgy of St. Cyril of Alexandria beautifully expresses the priest's reliance on the sacraments for strength:

> "Grant, O Lord, that through Your Body and Blood, we may be filled with the strength of Your Spirit, that we may overcome the temptations of the world, the flesh, and the devil. Cleanse us from all sin, and fortify us in this spiritual battle, that we may remain steadfast in our faith and devoted to Your holy will."

This prayer reflects the power of the Eucharist in strengthening the priest for his spiritual battles, as he draws directly from the life of Christ to overcome sin and temptation.

## The Support of the Church and the Communion of Saints

The priest does not fight his spiritual battles alone. He is supported by the prayers of the Church and the intercession of the saints, who accompany him in his struggles. The Church, as the Body of Christ, is a source of strength for the priest, offering him encouragement, support, and the prayers of the faithful. Additionally, the communion of saints, those holy men and women who have gone before him, provides the priest with a powerful source of intercession and inspiration in his trials.

St. John Chrysostom spoke of the priest's need for the prayers of the Church:

> "The priest, though he holds a high office, is still a man subject to weakness and temptation. He therefore needs the prayers of his people, that he may be strengthened in his ministry and protected from the assaults of the devil" (*On the Priesthood, Book IV*).

The priest is not invincible; he depends on the prayers of the faithful to help him fulfill his ministry and resist the temptations that threaten his soul.

The Divine Liturgy of St. Basil reflects this communal aspect of spiritual warfare:

> "We give thanks to You, O Lord, for the prayers of Your saints, who intercede for us and strengthen us in our time of need. Through their prayers and the prayers of Your Church, may we be delivered from all harm and preserved in holiness."

This prayer highlights the importance of the communion of saints in the priest's spiritual life, as their intercession strengthens him in his struggles and helps him to remain faithful to his calling.

## The Priest's Union with Christ in Suffering

The trials and struggles the priest endures draw him closer to Christ, who suffered for the sake of redeeming humanity. St. Peter exhorts believers, especially those in leadership, to see suffering as participation in Christ's own experience: "Rejoice to the extent that you partake of Christ's sufferings, that when His glory is revealed, you may also be glad with exceeding joy." (1 Peter 4:13). The priest's union with Christ in suffering is not a burden to be feared, but a grace to be embraced, for it deepens his communion with the Savior.

In embracing suffering, the priest also shares in Christ's redemptive mission. Just as the Apostle Paul viewed his own sufferings as filling up "what is lacking in the afflictions of Christ, for the sake of His body, which is the church" (Colossians 1:24), the priest's struggles are united with the redemptive work of Christ, bringing spiritual benefit to those he serves. Through the trials he endures, the priest becomes a witness to the faithful, demonstrating that victory is found not in avoiding suffering but in overcoming it through faith and trust in God.

## Growing in Humility through Trials

One of the hidden graces of enduring temptations and trials is the gift of humility. The priest, through his struggles, learns to rely more deeply on God's strength and less on his own abilities. St. James writes, "Humble yourselves in the sight of the Lord, and He will lift you up" (James 4:10). The priest's humility, cultivated through his experience of weakness, becomes an instrument of spiritual power, for in his dependence on God, he is made strong.

St. Paul's own experience illustrates this deep reliance on God, as he writes to the Corinthians: "For we do not want you to be ignorant, brothers, of the affliction we experienced in Asia. For we were so utterly burdened beyond our strength that we despaired of life itself" (2 Corinthians 1:8, ESV). This passage reveals how even the Apostle Paul, despite his great faith, encountered overwhelming challenges that drove him to depend fully on God's sustaining power. Similarly, the priest's trials teach him humility and deepen his trust in God's grace.

This humility is vital for the priest, as it prevents the growth of pride, which is one of the greatest dangers in spiritual ministry. St. Paul himself experienced a "thorn in the flesh" that kept him humble and reliant on God's grace despite the many spiritual gifts and revelations he had received (2 Corinthians 12:7-9). Likewise, the trials and temptations faced by the priest serve as reminders of his human frailty and his constant need for God's mercy and strength.

# The Role of the Holy Spirit in the Priest's Struggles

Throughout his trials, the priest is never alone. The Holy Spirit, the Comforter and Advocate, is always present to guide, strengthen, and console the priest in his moments of weakness. As Jesus promised His disciples before His ascension, "You shall receive power when the Holy Spirit has come upon you" (Acts 1:8), so too does the priest receive divine strength through the Spirit to face the challenges that come his way.

The Holy Spirit equips the priest with the gifts necessary for spiritual warfare: wisdom to discern the enemy's tactics, courage to stand firm in the truth, and perseverance to endure the trials that accompany their vocation. The priest is called to continually seek the Spirit's guidance in prayer, trusting in the Spirit's power to sustain him in every difficulty. As St. Paul encouraged the Romans, "The Spirit also helps in our weaknesses. For we do not know what we should pray for as we ought, but the Spirit Himself makes intercession for us with groanings which cannot be uttered" (Romans 8:26).

## Persevering in Hope

Ultimately, the priest's trials and struggles are not a sign of defeat but an opportunity for deeper reliance on God and growth in hope. The priest's hope is not in his ability to overcome temptation or endure suffering on his own but in the power of Christ, who works through him.

St. Paul offers words of encouragement to all believers who face trials, including the priest: "And not only that, but we also glory in tribulations, knowing that tribulation produces perseverance; and perseverance, character; and character, hope. Now hope does not disappoint, because the love of God has been poured out in our hearts by the Holy Spirit who was given to us" (Romans 5:3-5).

The priest's perseverance through spiritual warfare and trials is, ultimately, a testament to the love of God the Father, who sustains him through every difficulty. This love poured out through the Holy Spirit is what enables the priest to continue his mission, even in the face of great opposition. As the priest grows in hope, he also becomes a source of hope for the faithful, showing them that God's grace is sufficient in every struggle and that victory is assured in Christ.

## Conclusion

The priest's life, marked by temptations, trials, and spiritual warfare, is a profound reflection of God the Father's love and care, as revealed in Christ. Through his struggles, the priest grows in humility, reliance on God's grace, and spiritual maturity. He is never alone in his battles; the Holy Spirit empowers and sustains him, and the prayers of the Church and the saints fortify him. By embracing the cross of his vocation, the priest becomes a living witness to the power of Christ's victory over sin and death.

St. John Chrysostom's reflection on the priesthood captures the heart of this struggle:

> "Though the priest may face great struggles, temptations, and the attacks of the enemy, he is not left to fight alone. God's grace is sufficient, and His strength will uphold him in every trial."

The priest's ultimate triumph is not found in his own strength but in the grace of God, who equips him for every battle and leads him through every trial to the glory of the resurrection.

The priest's life of struggle is, therefore, not a life of defeat but a life of victory—a victory won through faith, perseverance, and the unshakable hope that God's love will never fail. Through his faithfulness in spiritual warfare, the priest becomes a beacon of hope and strength for the Church, leading the faithful toward the ultimate victory in Christ.

# Chapter 14

# Bearing the Cross with Christ

At the heart of the priestly ministry lies the call to live a life of sacrifice, following in the footsteps of Christ, who gave Himself completely for the salvation of the world. The priest is called to share in Christ's sacrificial love, offering his life in service to God and His people. This chapter examines the significance of sacrifice in the priest's life, the relationship between the priest's ministry and the cross of Christ, and how the priest can faithfully bear the cross in his daily ministry.

## A Call to Sacrificial Love

From the moment of ordination, the priest is set apart to live a life of sacrificial love, modeled on the example of Christ. Jesus said, "Greater love has no one than this than to lay down one's life for his friends" (John 15:13). Uniquely, the priest is called to lay down his life in service to others, following the example of Christ, the Good Shepherd, who gave His life for the sheep.

St. John Chrysostom emphasized the priest's call to sacrificial love:

> "The priest is called to be ready to give up everything for the sake of his people, just as Christ gave up everything for the sake of the world. His love must be selfless and unconditional, for it is through this love that the priest reflects the love of Christ." (*On the Priesthood, Book III*).

This sacrificial love goes beyond mere duty—it is a deep personal commitment to embody Christ's self-giving love.

The priest's sacrificial love manifests itself in small daily acts of self-denial. These acts may include giving up personal time and preferences or enduring challenges for the good of his parishioners. Each of these sacrifices, though small, become profound ways in which the priest shares in the love of Christ and grows in holiness, embodying Paul's call to live out Christ's love: "Let each of you look out not only for his own interests but also for the interests of others" (Philippians 2:4).

## The Priest and the Cross of Christ

The cross is central to the priest's identity and mission. Just as Christ bore the cross for the salvation of the world, the priest is called to bear his own cross in union with Christ. This involves accepting the hardships, challenges, and sufferings that come with ministry, not as obstacles but as opportunities to participate in the redemptive work of Christ.

St. Gregory the Great, in his *Pastoral Rule*, wrote:

> "The priest is called to be prepared to carry the cross of ministry, for his calling is not to comfort but to sacrifice. The cross may come in many forms, but in each one, the priest finds a deeper union with Christ, who suffered for the sake of love."

The cross that the priest bears may come in the form of the demands of ministry, personal sacrifices, or spiritual trials, yet in each of these, the priest is drawn closer to Christ.

Suffering in ministry becomes a means of spiritual growth, as St. Paul teaches that "tribulation produces perseverance; and perseverance, character; and character, hope." (Romans 5:3-4). Through these trials, the priest is conformed more fully to the image of Christ, growing in humility, compassion, and love. The priest's willingness to embrace the cross also serves as a powerful witness to his flock, showing them the path of discipleship.

## Sacrifice of the Eucharist and the Priest's Life

The priest's life of sacrifice is intimately connected to the Eucharist, the sacrament that makes present Christ's sacrifice on the cross. In each celebration of the Eucharist, the priest offers the Body and Blood of the Lord for the salvation of the world. This sacred act is not only liturgical but also a reflection of the priest's own call to live a life of self-offering.

St. John Chrysostom explained the profound connection between the Eucharist and the priest's life:

> "What the priest does at the altar, he must also do in his own life. Just as he offers Christ's Body and Blood for the salvation of the world, he must also offer his own life as a sacrifice for the people" (*Homilies on Hebrews*).

This highlights that the Eucharist is not just a ritual for the priest but a call to imitate Christ's self-offering in every aspect of life.

As the priest partakes in the Body and Blood of Christ, he draws spiritual nourishment from the Eucharist, which strengthens him in the face of challenges and renews his commitment to live a life of sacrifice. The Eucharist sustains the priest, reminding him of his call to offer himself as a living sacrifice, as St. Paul writes: "Present your bodies a living sacrifice, holy, acceptable to God, which is your reasonable service." (Romans 12:1).

## Sacrifices in Ministry: Self-Denial and Service

The priest's life of sacrifice is not only spiritual but also practical. In his daily ministry, the priest is called to practice self-denial and serve others, setting aside his own needs and desires for the good of the faithful. This practical self-denial reflects Christ's own words, "For even the Son of Man did not come to be served, but to serve, and to give His life a ransom for many" (Mark 10:45).

St. Gregory the Great, in his *Pastoral Rule,* emphasized the practical demands of the priest's sacrifices:

> "The priest's life is one of constant self-denial. Whether it be attending to the sick at all hours or offering counsel to those in need, the priest is called always to be willing to give of himself for the good of his people."

These acts of sacrifice are not burdens but opportunities for the priest to serve Christ by serving His people.

In a world that often prioritizes personal gain and comfort, the priest's willingness to lay down his life for others stands as a powerful testimony to the Gospel. His life of service points others to the sacrificial love of Christ and calls them to live lives of generosity, service, and self-giving.

## The Joy of Sacrifice

While the priest's life of sacrifice involves hardship, it is also filled with profound joy. This joy comes from sharing in the redemptive work of Christ and knowing that his sacrifices are not in vain but part of God's plan for the salvation of souls. Jesus promised, "Whoever desires to save his life will lose it, but whoever loses his life for My sake will find it" (Matthew 16:25), and this promise is fulfilled in the life of the priest, who finds joy in giving his life for others.

St. Gregory of Nazianzus spoke of the joy that comes from sacrificial love:

> "The priest's joy is not found in worldly pleasures but in the knowledge that he is participating in the saving work of Christ. His sacrifices, though difficult, become a source of grace and joy, for they are offered

out of love for God and His people" (*Oration 2, On the Priesthood*).

This joy is not fleeting but a deep and abiding sense of peace and fulfillment that comes from knowing that the priest's life is part of God's work of salvation.

## Finding Strength in Christ's Sacrifice

The priest cannot live a life of sacrifice by his own strength; he must draw his strength from Christ, who is the source of all grace. St. Paul's words to the Corinthians offer encouragement: "For the love of Christ compels us, because we judge thus: that if One died for all, then all died" (2 Corinthians 5:14). It is Christ's love that compels the priest to give of himself for others, and it is Christ's grace that sustains him in this sacrificial life.

Prayer is essential in sustaining the priest's life of sacrifice. In prayer, the priest encounters Christ, who renews and strengthens him. The priest's sacrifices, both large and small, are united with Christ's own sacrifice, and through this union, the priest finds the grace and strength to persevere in his ministry.

## Conclusion

The priest's life is one of sacrifice, in union with Christ, who gave Himself completely for the salvation of the world. Through daily acts of self-denial, service, and love, the priest participates in the redemptive work of Christ and finds joy in bearing the cross with Him. By drawing strength from the Eucharist, prayer, and the love of Christ, the priest is able to live out his calling with courage, perseverance, and joy.

The priest's sacrifices are not burdens to be avoided but gifts to be embraced, for in the act of giving, the priest becomes more fully conformed to the image of Christ. As he shares in Christ's sufferings, he also shares in His glory, experiencing the deep joy that comes from knowing his life is part of Christ's saving mission.

In embracing a life of sacrifice, the priest becomes a living sign of the Gospel, embodying the truth that true life is found not in self-preservation but in self-giving love. This life of sacrifice, though demanding, is filled with grace, meaning, and the profound joy that comes from living a life dedicated to the service of God and His people.

# Chapter 15

# The Priest's Spiritual Fruitfulness

Every priest's life leaves a lasting impact on the people and communities he serves. His spiritual fruitfulness is not measured by worldly success or personal achievements but by the foundation he builds in the hearts and minds of those entrusted to his care. As a spiritual father, the priest's influence extends beyond his years of active ministry, shaping the faith, values, and spiritual vitality of future generations. This chapter examines how the priest bears lasting spiritual fruit, the significance of mentorship and discipleship, and the enduring impact of a priest's dedication to their calling.

## The Priest as a Spiritual Father

From the moment of ordination, the priest assumes the role of a spiritual father to his flock. This fatherhood is not biological but spiritual, marked by the priest's responsibility to nurture the faith and spiritual growth of his parishioners. Like a father who raises his children, the priest is called to guide, protect, and instruct the faithful, helping them deepen their relationship with God.

St. John Chrysostom emphasized the profound spiritual fatherhood of the priest:

> "The priest is a father not by flesh but by spirit, for his task is to beget souls to Christ, to nurture them in the faith, and to guide them to salvation" (*On the Priesthood, Book III*).

This fatherly care, filled with love and dedication, is at the core of the priest's spiritual fruitfulness, as it shapes the lives of those he serves.

St. Paul also referred to himself as a spiritual father to the early Christian communities, writing to the Corinthians, "For though you might have ten thousand instructors in Christ, yet you do not have many fathers; for in Christ Jesus, I have begotten you through the gospel" (1 Corinthians 4:15). The priest, like Paul, acts as a spiritual father to his parish, providing guidance, instruction, and encouragement as they navigate their journey of faith.

## Teaching and Preaching: Planting Seeds of Faith

One of the primary ways the priest bears spiritual fruit is through his teaching and preaching. The priest is a sower of seeds, planting the Word of God in the hearts of his congregation. Each sermon, Bible study, and catechetical lesson serves as an opportunity to instruct, inspire, and deepen the faith of the people.

St. Gregory the Great highlighted the lasting impact of a priest's teaching:

> "The words of a priest, when spoken with truth and love, become seeds that take root in the hearts of the faithful. Though the priest may not always see the fruits of his labor, he must trust that God, in His time, will bring about the growth" (*Pastoral Rule*).

Like the sower in Jesus' parable (Matthew 13:3-9), the priest's task is to plant the seeds of faith, trusting that God will cause them to flourish.

By grounding his teaching in Scripture and the Church's Tradition, the priest helps build a firm foundation of faith in the lives of his parishioners. This spiritual fruitfulness endures, passing from one generation to the next, as the seeds of faith continue to grow long after the priest has moved on.

## Mentorship and Discipleship: Raising Up Future Leaders

Another vital aspect of the priest's spiritual fruitfulness is his role in raising up future shepherds within the Church. The priest's responsibility is not only to minister to his current congregation but also to mentor and disciple individuals who will carry forward the Church's mission in the future. By investing in the spiritual growth and leadership development of others, the priest ensures that the Church will continue to thrive long after his time in ministry has ended.

St. Paul modeled this approach to ministry by mentoring young shepherds, such as Timothy and Titus. He wrote to Timothy, "The things that you have heard from me among many witnesses commit these to faithful men who will be able to teach others also" (2 Timothy 2:2). The priest, like Paul, is called to entrust the faith to others, equipping them to serve as future shepherds, teachers, and evangelists.

St. John Chrysostom emphasized the importance of discipleship in the priest's ministry:

> "The priest is called not only to preach but must also form others who will preach, teaching them by word and example how to lead the people in holiness" (*On the Priesthood, Book VI*).

By raising up future shepherds, the priest multiplies his influence and extends his spiritual fruitfulness, ensuring that the Church's mission continues beyond his own ministry.

## Building Strong Communities of Faith

The priest's spiritual fruitfulness is also seen in the strength and vitality of the parish community he helps to build. A healthy, vibrant parish is one where the faithful are actively engaged in worship, service, and evangelization. The priest plays a critical role in fostering this type of community, providing guidance, vision, and spiritual nourishment that encourage the people to grow in their relationship with Christ and in their love for one another.

St. Basil's Divine Liturgy reflects the priest's role in building strong communities of faith:

> "O Lord, bless this Your Church, strengthen its people in love and unity, and guide Your servant in leading them to worship You in spirit and truth."

This prayer encapsulates the priest's responsibility to create a parish community where Christ is at the center and where the faithful are united in love and service.

The priest's efforts to build a strong community are an essential part of his spiritual fruitfulness. A vibrant parish continues to bear fruit long after the priest has moved on, as the spiritual foundation he has laid enables future generations to thrive in their faith.

# Personal Holiness: The Core of the Priest's Spiritual Fruitfulness

At the heart of the priest's spiritual fruitfulness is his personal holiness. The priest's example of living a life of prayer, humility, and virtue speaks louder than his words or actions. Parishioners are profoundly influenced by the priest's authenticity, integrity, and commitment to holiness. His life becomes a living testimony to the transformative power of the Gospel.

In John 17:19, Jesus prayed to the Father, "For their sakes I sanctify Myself, that they also may be sanctified by the truth." Here, Christ reveals the depth of His love and dedication, setting Himself apart for the sake of His disciples. This act of sanctification was not merely a ritual but a total dedication to

God's will, even to the point of sacrifice. Similarly, the priest is called to sanctify himself, dedicating his life wholly to God and His people so that through his example, others may be inspired to pursue holiness.

St. Gregory of Nazianzus emphasized the importance of personal holiness in the priest's ministry:

> "The priest is called first to be holy himself before he can lead others to holiness. His own life must reflect the virtues he preaches, for his actions speak louder than his words" (*Oration 2, On the Priesthood*).

The priest's pursuit of personal holiness serves as a beacon of light to his parish, inspiring others to seek holiness in their own lives.

Holiness is a daily striving to grow in love for God and neighbor. The priest's humility, willingness to acknowledge his own weaknesses, and reliance on God's grace serve as an example for the faithful. His prayer life, devotion to the sacraments, and love for the Church inspire others to cultivate a deeper relationship with God. Just as Christ's sanctification was for the benefit of His disciples, the priest's pursuit of holiness is a ministry of love, leading his parishioners closer to God through the truth of the Gospel.

## A Life of Love and Service

Ultimately, the priest's spiritual fruitfulness is rooted in a life of love and service. Jesus taught His disciples, "By this, all will know that you are My disciples if you have love for one another" (John 13:35). The priest's love for God and his people is the foundation of his ministry, and it is this love that leaves the deepest impression on the hearts of those he serves.

St. Cyril of Alexandria, in his liturgy, expresses the priest's call to love:

"O Lord, fill my heart with Your love, that I may serve Your people with joy and humility. Help me to be a faithful shepherd, guiding them in Your truth and leading them in Your love."

The priest's acts of love and service—whether they be pastoral care for the sick, comforting the grieving, or guiding the lost—are the building blocks of his spiritual fruitfulness.

As a servant of Christ, the priest's ultimate goal is not to build a legacy for himself but to point others toward the love and mercy of God. In this way, the priest's spiritual fruitfulness is not about personal recognition but about the souls he has guided toward eternal life.

## Conclusion

The priest's spiritual fruitfulness is built on the foundation of spiritual fatherhood, teaching, mentorship, community-building, personal holiness, and selfless love. By faithfully serving God and His people, the priest leaves behind a spiritual inheritance that continues to bear fruit for generations to come. His spiritual fruitfulness is not measured by worldly standards but by the lives he has touched, the faith he has nurtured, and the future shepherds he has raised up. In all of this, the priest's life points to Christ, the true source of all grace and the ultimate foundation upon which the Church is built.

# Bibliography

## Bible Translations:

- The Holy Bible: *Legacy Standard Bible (LSB)*. Steadfast Bibles, 2022.

- The Holy Bible: *New King James Version (NKJV)*. Thomas Nelson, 1982.

- The Holy Bible: *New International Version (NIV)*. Zondervan, 2011.

- The Holy Bible: *Revised Standard Version (RSV)*. Thomas Nelson & Sons, 1952.

- The Holy Bible: *English Standard Version (ESV)*. Crossway, 2001.

## Divine Liturgies:

- St. Basil the Great. *Divine Liturgy*. Translated by Archimandrite Ephrem. Greek Orthodox Archdiocese, 1995.

- St. Cyril of Alexandria. *Divine Liturgy*. Translated by Archimandrite Ephrem. Greek Orthodox Archdiocese, 1995.

- St. Gregory the Theologian, *Divine Liturgy*. Translated by Archimandrite Ephrem Lash. Holy Cross Orthodox Press, 2008.

- Serapion, H.E. Metropolitan, *The Divine Liturgy, the Anaphoras of Saints Basil, Gregory, and Cyril*. Coptic Orthodox Publishers, 2007

- Sleman, Hegumen Abraam, *St. Basil Liturgy, Reference Book*. CopticChurch.net

## Books and Commentaries:

- St. Ambrose of Milan. *On the Duties of the Clergy, Book II*. Translated by H. de Romestin. Nicene and Post-Nicene Fathers, Series II, Vol. 10. T&T Clark, 1896.

- St. Augustine. *Against Heresies, Book III*. Translated by John Hammond Taylor. Catholic University of America Press, 1956.

- St. Basil the Great. *Homilies on the Psalms.* Translated by C. Paul Schroeder. St. Vladimir's Seminary Press, 2005.

- St. Chrysostom, John. *Homilies on the Gospel of Matthew*. Translated by George Prevost. Nicene and Post-Nicene Fathers, Series I, Vol. 10. T&T Clark, 1888.

- St. Chrysostom, John. *Homilies on Hebrews*. Translated by William H. Payne. Nicene and Post-Nicene Fathers, Series I, Vol. 14. T&T Clark, 1889.

- St. Chrysostom, John. *Homilies on Acts*. Translated by J. Walker. Nicene and Post-Nicene Fathers, Series I, Vol. 11. T&T Clark, 1889.

- St. Cyril of Alexandria. *Homilies on the Gospel of John*. Translated by Philip E. Pusey. Oxford University Press, 1879.

- St. Gregory of Nazianzus. *Oration 2 on the Priesthood*. Translated by John A. McGuckin. St. Vladimir's Seminary Press, 2012.

- St. Gregory of Nazianzus. Oration 39, On the Feast of Theophany. Translated by Philip Schaff. Nicene and Post-Nicene Fathers, Series II, Vol. 7. T&T Clark, 1894.

- St. Irenaeus of Lyons. *Against Heresies, Book III*. Translated by Dominic J. Unger. Catholic University of America Press, 1992.

- St. Ignatius of Antioch. *Letter to the Smyrnaeans*. Translated by J. B. Lightfoot. Macmillan, 1891.

- St. Athanasius. *On the Incarnation*. Translated by John Behr. St. Vladimir's Seminary Press, 2011.

- St. Augustine. *Sermon on Pastors*. Translated by Edmund Hill. New City Press, 1990.

## Articles and Journals:

- Chan, Simon. *"The Theology of the Priesthood."* Journal of Ecclesiastical Studies 45, no. 3 (2001): 213-235.

- Pitre, Brant. *"The New Davidic Priest-King: Jesus and the Priesthood in the New Testament."* Catholic Biblical Quarterly 64, no. 3 (2002): 509-527.

www.ingramcontent.com/pod-product-compliance
Lightning Source LLC
Chambersburg PA
CBHW071141090426
42736CB00012B/2191